TOUSSAINT L'OUVERTURE

TOUSSAINT L'OUVERTURE

Thomas & Dorothy Hoobler

CHELSEA HOUSE PUBLISHERS
NEW YORK
PHILADELPHIA

Chelsea House Publishers
EDITOR-IN-CHIEF: Nancy Toff
EXECUTIVE EDITOR: Remmel T. Nunn
MANAGING EDITOR: Karyn Gullen Browne
COPY CHIEF: Juliann Barbato
PICTURE EDITOR: Adrian G. Allen
ART DIRECTOR: Maria Epes
MANUFACTURING MANAGER: Gerald Levine

World Leaders—Past & Present
SENIOR EDITOR: John W. Selfridge

Staff for TOUSSAINT L'OUVERTURE
ASSOCIATE EDITOR: Jeff Klein
DEPUTY COPY CHIEF: Nicole Bowen
EDITORIAL ASSISTANT: Nate Eaton
PICTURE RESEARCHER: Susan Biederman
ASSISTANT ART DIRECTOR: Loraine Machlin
DESIGNER: David Murray
DESIGN ASSISTANT: James Baker
PRODUCTION MANAGER: Joseph Romano
PRODUCTION COORDINATOR: Marie Claire Cebrián
COVER ILLUSTRATION: Rick Daskam

First Printing

1 3 5 7 9 8 6 4 2

Library of Congress Cataloging-in-Publication Data

Hoobler, Thomas.
    Toussaint L'Ouverture / Thomas & Dorothy Hoobler and Hoobler,
Dorothy.
    p. cm.—(World leaders past & present)
    Bibliography: p.
    Includes index.
    Summary: A biography of the eighteenth-century slave who led
his people in the struggle for an independent Haiti and became its
ruler in 1799.
    ISBN 1-55546-818-7
         0-7910-0705-7 (pbk.)
    1. Toussaint L'Ouverture, 1743?–1803—Juvenile literature.
2. Haiti—History—Revolution, 1791–1804—Juvenile literature.
3. Revolutionists—Haiti—Biography—Juvenile literature.
4. Generals—Haiti—Biography—Juvenile literature. [1. Toussaint
L'Ouverture, 1743?–1803. 2. Haiti—History—Revolution,
1791–1804. 3. Revolutionists. 4. Generals. 5. Blacks—Biography.]
I. Hoobler, Dorothy. II. Title. III. Series.
F1923.T69H66 1989
972.94'03'092—dc20   89-33123
[B]   CIP
[92]   AC

Contents

JOHN ADAMS
JOHN QUINCY ADAMS
KONRAD ADENAUER
ALEXANDER THE GREAT
SALVADOR ALLENDE
MARC ANTONY
CORAZON AQUINO
YASIR ARAFAT
KING ARTHUR
HAFEZ AL-ASSAD
KEMAL ATATÜRK
ATTILA
CLEMENT ATTLEE
AUGUSTUS CAESAR
MENACHEM BEGIN
DAVID BEN-GURION
OTTO VON BISMARCK
LÉON BLUM
SIMON BOLÍVAR
CESARE BORGIA
WILLY BRANDT
LEONID BREZHNEV
JULIUS CAESAR
JOHN CALVIN
JIMMY CARTER
FIDEL CASTRO
CATHERINE THE GREAT
CHARLEMAGNE
CHIANG KAI-SHEK
WINSTON CHURCHILL
GEORGES CLEMENCEAU
CLEOPATRA
CONSTANTINE THE GREAT
HERNÁN CORTÉS
OLIVER CROMWELL
GEORGES-JACQUES
    DANTON
JEFFERSON DAVIS
MOSHE DAYAN
CHARLES DE GAULLE
EAMON DE VALERA
EUGENE DEBS
DENG XIAOPING
BENJAMIN DISRAELI
ALEXANDER DUBČEK
FRANÇOIS & JEAN-CLAUDE
    DUVALIER
DWIGHT EISENHOWER
ELEANOR OF AQUITAINE
ELIZABETH I
FAISAL
FERDINAND & ISABELLA
FRANCISCO FRANCO
BENJAMIN FRANKLIN

FREDERICK THE GREAT
INDIRA GANDHI
MOHANDAS GANDHI
GIUSEPPE GARIBALDI
AMIN & BASHIR GEMAYEL
GENGHIS KHAN
WILLIAM GLADSTONE
MIKHAIL GORBACHEV
ULYSSES S. GRANT
ERNESTO "CHE" GUEVARA
TENZIN GYATSO
ALEXANDER HAMILTON
DAG HAMMARSKJÖLD
HENRY VIII
HENRY OF NAVARRE
PAUL VON HINDENBURG
HIROHITO
ADOLF HITLER
HO CHI MINH
KING HUSSEIN
IVAN THE TERRIBLE
ANDREW JACKSON
JAMES I
WOJCIECH JARUZELSKI
THOMAS JEFFERSON
JOAN OF ARC
POPE JOHN XXIII
POPE JOHN PAUL II
LYNDON JOHNSON
BENITO JUÁREZ
JOHN KENNEDY
ROBERT KENNEDY
JOMO KENYATTA
AYATOLLAH KHOMEINI
NIKITA KHRUSHCHEV
KIM IL SUNG
MARTIN LUTHER KING, JR.
HENRY KISSINGER
KUBLAI KHAN
LAFAYETTE
ROBERT E. LEE
VLADIMIR LENIN
ABRAHAM LINCOLN
DAVID LLOYD GEORGE
LOUIS XIV
MARTIN LUTHER
JUDAS MACCABEUS
JAMES MADISON
NELSON & WINNIE
    MANDELA
MAO ZEDONG
FERDINAND MARCOS
GEORGE MARSHALL

MARY, QUEEN OF SCOTS
TOMÁS MASARYK
GOLDA MEIR
KLEMENS VON METTERNICH
JAMES MONROE
HOSNI MUBARAK
ROBERT MUGABE
BENITO MUSSOLINI
NAPOLÉON BONAPARTE
GAMAL ABDEL NASSER
JAWAHARLAL NEHRU
NERO
NICHOLAS II
RICHARD NIXON
KWAME NKRUMAH
DANIEL ORTEGA
MOHAMMED REZA PAHLAVI
THOMAS PAINE
CHARLES STEWART
    PARNELL
PERICLES
JUAN PERÓN
PETER THE GREAT
POL POT
MUAMMAR EL-QADDAFI
RONALD REAGAN
CARDINAL RICHELIEU
MAXIMILIEN ROBESPIERRE
ELEANOR ROOSEVELT
FRANKLIN ROOSEVELT
THEODORE ROOSEVELT
ANWAR SADAT
HAILE SELASSIE
PRINCE SIHANOUK
JAN SMUTS
JOSEPH STALIN
SUKARNO
SUN YAT-SEN
TAMERLANE
MOTHER TERESA
MARGARET THATCHER
JOSIP BROZ TITO
TOUSSAINT L'OUVERTURE
LEON TROTSKY
PIERRE TRUDEAU
HARRY TRUMAN
QUEEN VICTORIA
LECH WALESA
GEORGE WASHINGTON
CHAIM WEIZMANN
WOODROW WILSON
XERXES
EMILIANO ZAPATA
ZHOU ENLAI

CHELSEA HOUSE PUBLISHERS

ON LEADERSHIP

Arthur M. Schlesinger, jr.

LEADERSHIP, it may be said, is really what makes the world go round. Love no doubt smooths the passage; but love is a private transaction between consenting adults. Leadership is a public transaction with history. The idea of leadership affirms the capacity of individuals to move, inspire, and mobilize masses of people so that they act together in pursuit of an end. Sometimes leadership serves good purposes, sometimes bad; but whether the end is benign or evil, great leaders are those men and women who leave their personal stamp on history.

Now, the very concept of leadership implies the proposition that individuals can make a difference. This proposition has never been universally accepted. From classical times to the present day, eminent thinkers have regarded individuals as no more than the agents and pawns of larger forces, whether the gods and goddesses of the ancient world or, in the modern era, race, class, nation, the dialectic, the will of the people, the spirit of the times, history itself. Against such forces, the individual dwindles into insignificance.

So contends the thesis of historical determinism. Tolstoy's great novel *War and Peace* offers a famous statement of the case. Why, Tolstoy asked, did millions of men in the Napoleonic Wars, denying their human feelings and their common sense, move back and forth across Europe slaughtering their fellows? "The war," Tolstoy answered, "was bound to happen simply because it was bound to happen." All prior history predetermined it. As for leaders, they, Tolstoy said, "are but the labels that serve to give a name to an end and, like labels, they have the least possible connection with the event." The greater the leader, "the more conspicuous the inevitability and the predestination of every act he commits." The leader, said Tolstoy, is "the slave of history."

Determinism takes many forms. Marxism is the determinism of class. Nazism the determinism of race. But the idea of men and women as the slaves of history runs athwart the deepest human instincts. Rigid determinism abolishes the idea of human freedom—

the assumption of free choice that underlies every move we make, every word we speak, every thought we think. It abolishes the idea of human responsibility, since it is manifestly unfair to reward or punish people for actions that are by definition beyond their control. No one can live consistently by any deterministic creed. The Marxist states prove this themselves by their extreme susceptibility to the cult of leadership.

More than that, history refutes the idea that individuals make no difference. In December 1931 a British politician crossing Park Avenue in New York City between 76th and 77th Streets around 10:30 P.M. looked in the wrong direction and was knocked down by an automobile—a moment, he later recalled, of a man aghast, a world aglare: "I do not understand why I was not broken like an eggshell or squashed like a gooseberry." Fourteen months later an American politician, sitting in an open car in Miami, Florida, was fired on by an assassin; the man beside him was hit. Those who believe that individuals make no difference to history might well ponder whether the next two decades would have been the same had Mario Constasino's car killed Winston Churchill in 1931 and Giuseppe Zangara's bullet killed Franklin Roosevelt in 1933. Suppose, in addition, that Adolf Hitler had been killed in the street fighting during the Munich *Putsch* of 1923 and that Lenin had died of typhus during World War I. What would the 20th century be like now?

For better or for worse, individuals do make a difference. "The notion that a people can run itself and its affairs anonymously," wrote the philosopher William James, "is now well known to be the silliest of absurdities. Mankind does nothing save through initiatives on the part of inventors, great or small, and imitation by the rest of us—these are the sole factors in human progress. Individuals of genius show the way, and set the patterns, which common people then adopt and follow."

Leadership, James suggests, means leadership in thought as well as in action. In the long run, leaders in thought may well make the greater difference to the world. But, as Woodrow Wilson once said, "Those only are leaders of men, in the general eye, who lead in action. . . . It is at their hands that new thought gets its translation into the crude language of deeds." Leaders in thought often invent in solitude and obscurity, leaving to later generations the tasks of imitation. Leaders in action—the leaders portrayed in this series—have to be effective in their own time.

And they cannot be effective by themselves. They must act in response to the rhythms of their age. Their genius must be adapted, in a phrase of William James's, "to the receptivities of the moment." Leaders are useless without followers. "There goes the mob," said the French politician hearing a clamor in the streets. "I am their leader. I must follow them." Great leaders turn the inchoate emotions of the mob to purposes of their own. They seize on the opportunities of their time, the hopes, fears, frustrations, crises, potentialities. They succeed when events have prepared the way for them, when the community is awaiting to be aroused, when they can provide the clarifying and organizing ideas. Leadership ignites the circuit between the individual and the mass and thereby alters history.

It may alter history for better or for worse. Leaders have been responsible for the most extravagant follies and most monstrous crimes that have beset suffering humanity. They have also been vital in such gains as humanity has made in individual freedom, religious and racial tolerance, social justice, and respect for human rights.

There is no sure way to tell in advance who is going to lead for good and who for evil. But a glance at the gallery of men and women in *World Leaders—Past and Present* suggests some useful tests.

One test is this: Do leaders lead by force or by persuasion? By command or by consent? Through most of history leadership was exercised by the divine right of authority. The duty of followers was to defer and to obey. "Theirs not to reason why / Theirs but to do and die." On occasion, as with the so-called enlightened despots of the 18th century in Europe, absolutist leadership was animated by humane purposes. More often, absolutism nourished the passion for domination, land, gold, and conquest and resulted in tyranny.

The great revolution of modern times has been the revolution of equality. The idea that all people should be equal in their legal condition has undermined the old structure of authority, hierarchy, and deference. The revolution of equality has had two contrary effects on the nature of leadership. For equality, as Alexis de Tocqueville pointed out in his great study *Democracy in America*, might mean equality in servitude as well as equality in freedom.

"I know of only two methods of establishing equality in the political world," Tocqueville wrote. "Rights must be given to every citizen, or none at all to anyone . . . save one, who is the master of all." There was no middle ground "between the sovereignty of all and the absolute power of one man." In his astonishing prediction of 20th-century totalitarian dictatorship, Tocqueville explained how the revolution of equality could lead to the *"Führerprinzip"* and more terrible absolutism than the world had ever known.

But when rights are given to every citizen and the sovereignty of all is established, the problem of leadership takes a new form, becomes more exacting than ever before. It is easy to issue commands and enforce them by the rope and the stake, the concentration camp and the *gulag*. It is much harder to use argument and achievement to overcome opposition and win consent. The Founding Fathers of the United States understood the difficulty. They believed that history had given them the opportunity to decide, as Alexander Hamilton wrote in the first Federalist Paper, whether men are indeed capable of basing government on "reflection and choice, or whether they are forever destined to depend . . . on accident and force."

Government by reflection and choice called for a new style of leadership and a new quality of followership. It required leaders to be responsive to popular concerns, and it required followers to be active and informed participants in the process. Democracy does not eliminate emotion from politics; sometimes it fosters demagoguery; but it is confident that, as the greatest of democratic leaders put it, you cannot fool all of the people all of the time. It measures leadership by results and retires those who overreach or falter or fail.

It is true that in the long run despots are measured by results too. But they can postpone the day of judgment, sometimes indefinitely, and in the meantime they can do infinite harm. It is also true that democracy is no guarantee of virtue and intelligence in government, for the voice of the people is not necessarily the voice of God. But democracy, by assuring the right of opposition, offers built-in resistance to the evils inherent in absolutism. As the theologian Reinhold Niebuhr summed it up, "Man's capacity for justice makes democracy possible, but man's inclination to injustice makes democracy necessary."

A second test for leadership is the end for which power is sought. When leaders have as their goal the supremacy of a master race or the promotion of totalitarian revolution or the acquisition and exploitation of colonies or the protection of greed and privilege or the preservation of personal power, it is likely that their leadership will do little to advance the cause of humanity. When their goal is the abolition of slavery, the liberation of women, the enlargement of opportunity for the poor and powerless, the extension of equal rights to racial minorities, the defense of the freedoms of expression and opposition, it is likely that their leadership will increase the sum of human liberty and welfare.

Leaders have done great harm to the world. They have also conferred great benefits. You will find both sorts in this series. Even "good" leaders must be regarded with a certain wariness. Leaders are not demigods; they put on their trousers one leg after another just like ordinary mortals. No leader is infallible, and every leader needs to be reminded of this at regular intervals. Irreverence irritates leaders but is their salvation. Unquestioning submission corrupts leaders and demeans followers. Making a cult of a leader is always a mistake. Fortunately hero worship generates its own antidote. "Every hero," said Emerson, "becomes a bore at last."

The signal benefit the great leaders confer is to embolden the rest of us to live according to our own best selves, to be active, insistent, and resolute in affirming our own sense of things. For great leaders attest to the reality of human freedom against the supposed inevitabilities of history. And they attest to the wisdom and power that may lie within the most unlikely of us, which is why Abraham Lincoln remains the supreme example of great leadership. A great leader, said Emerson, exhibits new possibilities to all humanity. "We feed on genius. . . . Great men exist that there may be greater men."

Great leaders, in short, justify themselves by emancipating and empowering their followers. So humanity struggles to master its destiny, remembering with Alexis de Tocqueville: "It is true that around every man a fatal circle is traced beyond which he cannot pass; but within the wide verge of that circle he is powerful and free; as it is with man, so with communities."

1

The Coming of the Liberator

On April 14, 1798, the people of Port-au-Prince, the capital city of St. Domingue, turned out for a triumphal parade. The day was bright and sunny, and the blue waters of the Caribbean lapped against the shores of the French colony. All morning long, the news had spread through the city: The Liberator was coming!

Shortly after noon, a line of mounted soldiers rode into the city. They were dragoons, and they wore the bright blue uniforms of France, with highly polished cuirasses, or body armor, around their chests. Only one thing distinguished this line of smartly dressed dragoons from the forces of General Napoleon Bonaparte, who now commanded the armies of France in Europe. The short, gray-haired man at the head of the line, wearing the full-dress uniform of a French general, was black — as were most of the mounted troops he led.

I was born a slave, but nature gave me a soul of a free man. Every day I raised up my hands in prayer to God to implore him to come to the aid of my brethren and to shed the light of his mercy upon them.
—TOUSSAINT L'OUVERTURE
August 1797

A contemporary depiction of Toussaint L'Ouverture, the leader of the Haitian Revolution. From 1791 to 1802, Toussaint's troops, composed mostly of former slaves, defeated local forces and the armies of France, Spain, and Britain in the world's only successful slave rebellion.

13

The man riding at the head of the line was Toussaint L'Ouverture, and at that moment he was the virtual ruler of the colony where he had been born a slave about 55 years before. In the previous seven years, he had led the first successful slave revolt in history. And now, because he had driven off a British army that sought to seize France's richest colony, Toussaint was being cheered by the slaveholders themselves.

Awaiting his arrival in the city's main square were the mayor and the leading citizens. Around them were French priests in beautifully embroidered vestments and altar boys who swung smoking censers of fragrant incense. One held high a silver crucifix bearing the figure of Christ.

Toussaint rode toward them, through a triumphal arch of green branches and flowers. "*Vive Toussaint!*" cheered the crowd; "*Vive le Général! Vive le Libérateur!*" When he came to a line of young girls carrying baskets of flowers, he stopped, dismounted, and took a flower. Toussaint smiled and thanked the girls. Then, his spurs jangling in the dusty street, he walked to the welcoming party and knelt before the crucifix.

The mayor began a speech of praise and welcome. Four of Port-au-Prince's richest citizens rushed forward with a golden canopy to hold over Toussaint and shield him from the hot sun. Others prostrated themselves at his feet. Toussaint recognized the faces of his former enemies among the assemblage.

Toussaint seldom let his feelings show, confiding in neither friend nor enemy. On this occasion, however, his anger flared. He waved away the canopy and stepped back from the group of rich men. The mayor's speech halted, and the crowd heard Toussaint say, "A canopy and incense belong to God alone." Turning his heel on the welcoming party, he strode toward the government building at the edge of the square. His dragoons formed a line at the entrance to keep the crowd back, and Toussaint ran up the steps and disappeared inside.

That night, he reappeared for the gala ball and banquet that had been prepared. The richest whites in the city brought their wives and daughters to get

Toussaint is a negro and in the jargon of war has been called a brigand. But according to all accounts he is a negro born to vindicate the claims of this species and to show that the character of men is independent of color.
—LONDON GAZETTE
December 12, 1798

14

a closer look at the former slave who was now the virtual ruler of St. Domingue. He sipped his wine with the others, watched the men and women in silken suits and gowns perform the elaborate steps of a gavotte, and kept his thoughts to himself.

Elsewhere in the city that night, in little shacks by the swampy harbor, there were other dances and celebrations. In those narrow streets lived the blacks — those who felt real joy at his arrival. From their humble houses came the aroma of goat and chicken simmering in great iron pots. The songs they sang that night were not melodies from European drawing rooms. They were songs remembered from Africa, the homeland of their ancestors. Drums pounded out the rhythms that freed the bodies that had labored for so long under the whips of slaveholders. The Liberator had arrived!

An early 19th-century scene by the artist A. Brunias depicts village life in St. Domingue, as Haiti was called before 1804. The black majority in St. Domingue rallied under Toussaint's leadership and welcomed him as a liberator when he entered the capital city of Port-au-Prince in 1798.

2

The Centaur of the Plains

The island on which Toussaint was born was the second place Christopher Columbus saw when he discovered the New World in 1492. The native people — Columbus dubbed them Indians in his mistaken belief that he had reached the islands off the coast of China known as the East Indies — called their island Haïti, which means "mountainous." Columbus named it Hispaniola, in honor of the Spanish monarchs who had paid for his voyage.

The Indians of Haiti, who called themselves the Arawak and the Taino, welcomed Columbus — an act they soon came to regret. The Spaniards who followed in Columbus's wake during the next few years made slaves of the island's people, putting them to work mining gold for Spain. The Indians had no defense against the Spaniards' superior weapons — nor were they able to resist the European diseases that soon spread through the population. In the space of a single generation, the Indian population of the island shrank from about 1 million to about 60,000. Within a hundred years the Indians of Haiti disappeared altogether.

> *There is nothing which contributes more to the development of the colonies and the cultivation of their soil than the laborious toil of the negroes.*
> —LOUIS XIV
> 1670

Christopher Columbus arrives on the island of Hispaniola, his second landfall during his discovery of the New World in 1492. The half million Arawak and Taino Indians, some of whom are shown here greeting Columbus, were wiped out within 100 years through enslavement, massacre, and disease.

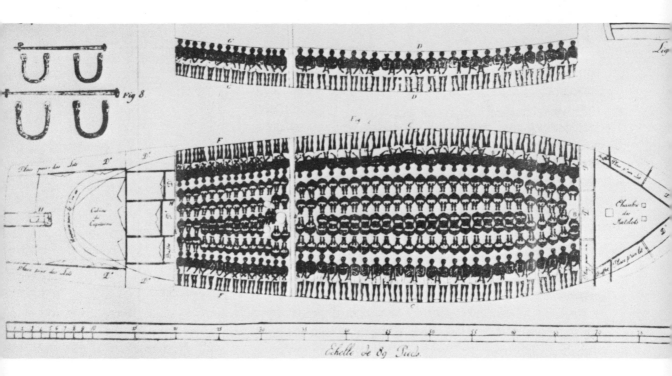

Echelle de 89 Pieds

An 18th-century diagram of the hold of a slave ship that transported hundreds of slaves from Africa. In the 1500s, Spain began the slave trade from Africa to the New World to supply labor for plantations in its Hispaniola colony of Santo Domingo. The French acquired the western half of the island in 1697 and stepped up the slave trade.

To replace the Indian labor, the Spaniards imported African slaves. In 1517, Spanish ships brought 15,000 slaves from Africa — the first to come to the New World. More were soon on their way, stuffed into the holds of slave ships so tightly that there was not even room for them to stand. The foul air and filth below decks were indescribable, and many slaves died on the journey across the Atlantic. Occasionally, ship captains let them come on deck for a few minutes of fresh air; but even in chains, many slaves would leap over the side of the ship, preferring drowning to the misery that awaited them below. Only the strongest survived the horrors of the Middle Passage.

With the discovery of far greater deposits of gold and silver in Mexico and Peru, Hispaniola lost many of its Spanish settlers. But before long, the island attracted other Europeans. Just north of Hispaniola lies the small island of Tortuga. It was used as a base by French pirates, who lay in wait for treasure-laden Spanish ships. Because the pirates ate smoked meat prepared in a process known by the Indian word *boucan*, they came to be called buccaneers.

Some of the buccaneers moved to Hispaniola. A visitor to the island said they looked like "the butcher's vilest servants, who have been eight days in the slaughterhouse without washing themselves." Nevertheless, the buccaneers' reports of Hispaniola's lushness reached the French king, who in 1665 sent a representative, Bertrand d'Ogeron, to the island.

D'Ogeron established a permanent French settlement on the western end of Hispaniola. The Spanish gold mines were at the eastern end, but the French were to show that the island's real wealth was in its rich farmland. During the next ten years, d'Ogeron encouraged people to come from France to establish plantations.

Men seeking a new life — prisoners, the poor — were not hard to find, but few women wanted to leave France for the Caribbean, where the climate was uncomfortably hot. So d'Ogeron brought prostitutes and female orphans to marry the male settlers. The marriage ceremonies included an unusual vow: "I take thee without knowing or caring to know, who thou art. . . . Give me only thy word for the future. I acquit thee of what is past."

Future slaves are led through the grasslands of West Africa en route to the ships that will take them to St. Domingue. Arabs, Europeans, and black Africans captured the slaves and sold them to the French, Spanish, Portuguese, British, and Americans, who then exploited their labor throughout the New World.

A depiction of a St. Domingue plantation in 1681. By the mid-1700s, the colony was France's richest overseas possession, and the exports from its sugar, indigo, cotton, and coffee plantations provided one-third of France's revenues.

The French found slavery as lucrative and convenient a form of labor as the Spaniards had. France's king Louis XIII had legalized slavery in 1633, justifying his action by saying that Christians could thus rescue Africans from idolatry and save their souls for Christ. But in reality, the life of a slave was miserable and brutal. Sold to the highest bidders at auctions in the slave bazaars of the island's ports, their mouths were forced open so their teeth could be examined — a way of determining their age. They were property and as such were treated like farm animals, without rights or the slightest dignity. A visitor to the island reported that one of his daughters was shocked to see that the slaves serving dinner wore no clothing. Their owner laughed at this idea, asking the girl if she would like him to dress his cattle and horses as well.

Overseers drove the slaves as long as there was light in the sky, which meant that at harvest time they worked 14 to 16 hours a day. Any slave who paused to rest immediately felt the sting of the overseer's lash. For those who dared to resist, there were fiendish punishments and tortures. Some were spread-eagled on the ground and whipped without mercy. Salt, pepper, lime, or boiling liquids were poured onto their wounds. Their feet were thrust into red-hot coals. Other slaves were smeared with molasses and buried in anthills. Tied on the ground, they were set upon by vicious dogs. Some were burned alive or stuffed with gunpowder and then blown to bits with the touch of a match.

White planters witness the punishment of slaves in the central square of Port-au-Prince in 1780. Backbreaking labor, squalid conditions, brutal punishments, and frequent mass executions killed tens of thousands of slaves each year on St. Domingue. It is estimated that the colony's black population of 500,000 had to be replaced every 20 years.

After a war between France and Spain in Europe, the Spanish ceded the western part of the island to France in 1697. Called St. Domingue by the French, the colony became a source of immense profit. Ships from French ports such as Marseille sailed to Africa, picked up a cargo of slaves, dropped them in St. Domingue, and returned with their holds filled with the products of St. Domingue's plantations — sugar, coffee, tobacco, and cocoa, all of which found eager buyers in Europe. St. Domingue became by far the most profitable of France's overseas possessions.

The French planters on the island lived in profuse luxury. A common French phrase of the time was "rich as a Creole." (*Creole* was the name for those who were born on the island — both blacks and whites — but it is often used only for those of European ancestry.) They were surrounded by slaves who, as one Frenchman wrote, "await the orders and even the lifted finger of a lone individual. . . . To have four times as many servants as one needs marks the grandiloquence of a wealthy man."

Yet most Creoles looked forward to the day when they could take the fortunes they had amassed and return to France. Women in particular were bored with the empty lives they led. A daughter of one planter wrote: "Have pity on us for an existence cut off from the world. We are . . . surrounded by over 200 slaves, the domestics alone amounting to 30. From morning to night their faces stare at us . . . and they are involved in the least details of our intimate existence. Our talk is taken up with the health of the slaves, the care they require, their schemes for revolt, and all our lives are bound up with these wretched beings."

Into this world arrived Toussaint's father, the son of an African chief. He had the good fortune to be bought by a relatively humane nobleman, the Comte de Noé. On his plantation, called Breda, the Comte encouraged his slaves to practice his own Catholic religion, granting them days off on religious holidays. Recognizing that Toussaint's father was a talented individual, the Comte gave him a small plot of land of his own to farm. Soon the slave married another slave of the plantation, and together they raised a family of eight children.

Their firstborn son, named François-Dominique Toussaint à Breda, was a small, sickly child. The other children of the plantation called him the Stick. The exact year of his birth is not known for certain, though 1743 or 1744 are likely dates.

From his earliest days, the young Toussaint was a loner. His father's privileged position gave Toussaint the freedom to wander through the woods and mountains near the plantation. He gathered flowers and herbs, learning their uses for healing. His father told him tales of the great days in Africa when his people were royalty.

Toussaint worked hard to overcome his physical weakness, swimming in the rivers, climbing the mountains, and learning to ride horses. By the time he was 12, he was renowned for his riding skills; his short, bowlegged body fit the back of a horse so snugly that the two looked as if they were born together. Riding mile upon mile through the fields and grasslands of the northern part of the island, he earned a new nickname: the Centaur of the Plains.

A St. Domingue market scene in the late 1700s. Slaves composed almost 90 percent of the colony's population, the remainder being made up of wealthy white plantation owners, a white merchant class, a small number of free blacks, and a sizable number of mulattoes (people of mixed black and white ancestry), many of whom were themselves wealthy slaveholders and merchants.

With equal determination, Toussaint gained an education that was to set him apart from others in his later years. His first teacher was a black man named Pierre Baptiste, who had served as godfather when Toussaint was baptized a Catholic at birth. Baptiste was to remain by Toussaint's side as a trusted adviser for the rest of his life.

Slaves arriving in St. Domingue spoke African languages. To communicate with each other and with their masters, they gradually learned Krayol, or Creole, a simple form of French mixed with bits of African languages. As Toussaint grew older, Baptiste taught him to speak formal French and introduced him to a French priest at the hospital where Baptiste worked.

The French priest, struck by Toussaint's intelligence, took the boy on as a student and taught him how to read and write. The French overseer of Breda allowed Toussaint to use his library, and gradually the young man learned of the history and culture of Europe, whose people had enslaved his own. He studied Julius Caesar's accounts of his military campaigns and voraciously read the histories of other famous generals, such as Alexander the Great.

Few black slaves were ever permitted to gain an education such as Toussaint had. Government policy stated that "the security of the whites demands that we keep the Negroes in the most profound ignorance." Indeed, when a Frenchman visiting Breda saw Toussaint sitting quietly reading a book, he was so enraged by the sight that he struck the book from Toussaint's hands and beat him until the boy's coat was stained with blood. Toussaint did not resist, but he saved the coat to remind himself of the incident.

That was always Toussaint's way. His mildness and self-control sometimes deceived those who did not know him well. He always tried to avoid violence, but when action was necessary he became ruthless. For much of his life, he observed the world around him. He saved in his memory all that he had seen and read, and when he finally acted, he astonished the world with his talent and skills.

When Toussaint was about 13, a one-armed black slave named Mackandal sought to organize a slave rebellion throughout the colony. He traveled to many plantations, slipping into slave quarters at night. Known as a *bokor*, or sorcerer-priest possessed of magical powers, Mackandal promised freedom. He told the slaves that on a certain day they should rise up, poison their masters, and take control of the plantations. Mackandal derived his power as a bokor from Voodoo, the religion the slaves brought with them from West Africa. Voodoo (the word means "spirit"), while recognizing the existence of one God, consists of the summoning of various good and evil spirits that worshipers believe exist everywhere in the world. The slaves treasured Voodoo as the lone aspect of their life that the whites were unable to touch. Indeed, the slaveholders and colonial authorities tried to outlaw the religion by imposing strict punishments on its practitioners, but the vast majority of blacks held to their belief in Voodoo.

Mackandal spread the word of his rebellion during Voodoo ceremonies, which were held in secret and at night to avoid detection by the whites. According to the black West Indian historian C. L. R. James, Mackandal

> aimed at delivering his people through poison. For six years he built up his organization, he and his followers poisoning not only whites but disobedient members of their own band. Then he arranged that on a particular day the water of every house in the capital of [Limbé] province was to be poisoned, and the general attack made on the whites while they were in the convulsions and anguish of death. He . . . arranged for bands of Negroes to leave the town and spread over the plains to massacre the whites.

Mackandal's rebellion resulted in the death of about 6,000 people, both black and white, but it failed to become the general massacre of whites its leader had envisioned. Finally Mackandal himself was captured and sentenced to be burned at the

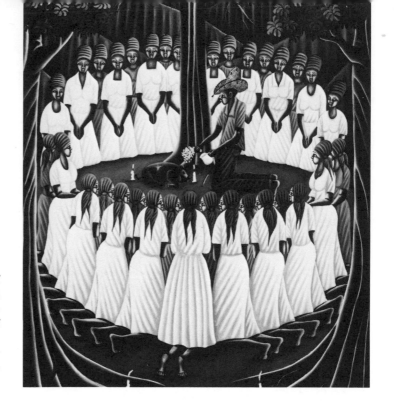

A modern Haitian painting of a Voodoo ceremony. Derived from West African spirit worship, Voodoo, the religion of St. Domingue's blacks, served as a rallying point for slave rebellions against the white plantation owners.

stake in the public square of Cap François in 1758. The flames destroyed his bonds before his life, and he jerked away from the stake and ran until he fell lifeless before the crowd. The blacks whispered to each other that the bokor had shown that the flames could not harm him; though his body died, they believed Mackandal would wake up in Africa, the homeland.

As Toussaint grew to young manhood, he became a servant within the Breda household. As a coach driver, he accompanied his master to the nearby city of Cap François (known as Le Cap; today it is called Cap Haitien), where French planters enjoyed parties and lavish banquets. Sitting with the other servants and observing the life of the city, Toussaint learned more about the complicated society of the colony of St. Domingue.

At the top of society were the *grands blancs* (great whites), who were the wealthy plantation owners and the members of the colonial government controlled by France. Below them were the white tradespeople and shop owners who came from every country in Europe. This lower class of whites was known as the *petits blancs,* or "little whites."

Skin color alone made the petits blancs superior to a sizable portion of St. Domingue's citizens, known as mulattoes, who numbered among their ancestors both blacks and whites. White slaveholders commonly used their female slaves to satisfy their sexual desires; the children of these unions were often granted their freedom, and many managed to become wealthy. Some mulattoes owned plantations that rivaled in size those owned by the grands blancs, and they too kept slaves.

With the matter of race permeating every aspect of Haitian society, the whites never accepted the mulattoes as equals; the wealthiest, most educated mulatto could not eat at the same table with the lowliest of the petits blancs. The colony had laws forbidding mulattoes to wear certain kinds and colors of clothes that whites reserved for themselves. Mulattoes who served in the military wore a different uniform from whites, and advancement to the highest ranks was denied them. The mulattoes seethed at their inferior status, and they most often vented their resentment not on the whites, but on the black slaves. Mulatto plantation owners treated their slaves as cruelly as the whites did; mulattoes as a group were adamantly opposed to any proposals to grant slaves even the most basic of human rights.

A view of the northern city of Cap François (also known as Le Cap), St. Domingue's leading port. In 1758 a Voodoo priest and slave named Mackandal led a slave uprising in the northern province that was crushed only after 6,000 people had been killed. Mackandal was executed in the city's main square.

All the wealth of France's richest colony rested on the forced labor of those at the bottom of the social pyramid. At the time of Toussaint's birth, there were 40,000 whites in the colony — about evenly divided between the grands and petits blancs. The mulattoes numbered about 23,000. Serving all of them were at least 500,000 blacks.

Not all blacks in St. Domingue were slaves. A very small number had gained their freedom — usually by buying it from their owners — and blended in with the mulatto population. However, thousands of others had fled their harsh masters and lived in the wild forests and mountain areas. The French and English called these escaped slaves *maroons*, a word derived from *marrons*, the Spanish term for domestic animals that had escaped and reverted to their wild state. The maroons managed to survive in the wilderness, raising families and practicing Voodoo in well-organized and well-defended villages. Maroon bands came down from the mountains to raid plantations, and some became so effective and powerful at it that the white authorities were forced to conclude treaties with them.

Toussaint as a young man, reading the work of the French philosopher Abbé Raynal. Born François-Dominique Toussaint à Breda, in 1743 or 1744, Toussaint was taught how to read and write by a French priest — even though slaves were forbidden by law from learning such skills — and became a talented writer, well versed in literature.

Abbé Raynal, the mid-17th-century French philosopher and Roman Catholic priest whose books opposing slavery deeply influenced Toussaint. "Natural liberty is the right which is given to all," wrote Raynal, who predicted that a black "man of courage" would soon would appear to "raise the sacred standard of liberty."

Meanwhile, Toussaint continued to serve his master loyally and well. He married Susannah, a slave woman of Breda who already had a son of her own. She bore another by Toussaint, but he loved both boys equally, and they had a happy family life. Like his own father, Toussaint had special privileges on the plantation, and his duties multiplied until he was a trusted steward.

Toussaint continued to read all the books he could get his hands on, and he learned that there were whites who opposed slavery. One of them, the Abbé Raynal, had written a book that fell into Toussaint's hands. Toussaint read these words of a white Frenchman, a priest: "Natural liberty is the right which is given to all. . . . [For the blacks] a man of courage, a leader only is [needed]. . . . Where is he? He will appear, we cannot doubt it. He will come and raise the sacred standard of liberty. . . . The name of the hero who will have established the rights of the human race will be blessed by all."

Toussaint was to be that hero. But his time had not yet come. Before it did, a revolution would break out in France itself, one that would have far-reaching consequences for Toussaint and all the people of St. Domingue.

3

"I Am Toussaint L'Ouverture"

In September 1789, a ship from France brought to St. Domingue the news of the storming of the Paris prison known as the Bastille — the start of the French Revolution.

Conditions in France were ripe for change. The gap between rich and poor was enormous. At the French court, King Louis XVI and his nobles lived in almost inconceivable luxury, while in the narrow streets of Paris the poorest of the king's subjects dressed in rags and begged for bread. Peasants in the French countryside barely scratched out a living.

Against this backdrop, the new ideas of the Enlightenment were hotly discussed in cafés and universities throughout France. The Enlightenment was an intellectual movement that spread through Europe in the 18th century. One of its central ideas was that there were laws of human behavior — as true as the principles of science. Some Enlightenment thinkers, such as Denis Diderot, felt that slavery was an unnatural condition, both for slaves and

Toussaint is the first and greatest of West Indians
—C. L. R. JAMES
Toussaint biographer

A cartoon drawn at the start of the French Revolution in 1789. It caricatures the three major class divisions then existing in French society by showing the nobles and clergy riding on the back of the peasants. The Revolution's ideals of liberty, equality, and fraternity soon spread to St. Domingue, inspiring the slaves there to revolt.

The storming of the Bastille by a Paris mob on July 14, 1789, marked the beginning of the French Revolution, in which the monarchy and its allies in the church and the nobility were overthrown by the masses.

slaveholders. Urging the abolition of slavery, Diderot wrote, "Let the colonies be destroyed rather than be the cause of so much evil." In 1788, Les Amis des Noirs, or The Friends of the Blacks, was formed in Paris to work for the rights of mulattoes and blacks. One of its members was the Abbé Raynal, whose writings had inspired Toussaint.

More practical reasons — lack of money and the need to raise taxes — caused King Louis XVI to call a meeting of the Estates General of France. This legislative body consisted of three branches, or estates. The first estate was composed of representatives of France's Catholic clergy, the second hereditary nobility, and the third represented the

rest of the people — about 95 percent of all French citizens.

In the Estates General, each branch had equal power. Thus, the common people were powerless against the combined power of clergy and nobility. On this occasion, however, the members of the third estate declared the establishment of a National Assembly, in which each representative's vote would be equal. When the king's soldiers locked them out of their meeting hall, the representatives of the third estate gathered at a nearby tennis court. There, on June 20, 1789, they took an oath — called the Tennis Court Oath — to remain in session until a new constitution was written for France.

A majority of the first estate joined the National Assembly. The king gave in and ordered the nobility to meet with it as well. In a dramatic session, aristocrats renounced their special privileges. Without bloodshed, France seemed to have undergone a peaceful revolution.

The people of Paris could not restrain their joy, nor their anger at the old regime. A mob of Parisians stormed the Bastille, a symbol of the privileges of the past. Though the first stage of the revolution had been peaceful, radicals would later use the Paris mob to carry it much further.

On August 26, the Assembly adopted the Declaration of the Rights of Man and the Citizen. Among other things, the declaration stated, "All men are born and live free and equal in their rights." This simple statement, like similar ones in the American Declaration of Independence, was subject to different interpretations.

An antislavery lithograph of the French revolutionary era protesting the 100-year-old *code noir*, or black code, that legally reduced blacks to the status of property. In the caption, the slave tells the white Frenchman, "I am a man, and nothing human is foreign to me."

Moi Egal à toi.
Couleur n'est rien, le cœur est tout ;
n'est tu pas mon frère ?

A poster of the kind often used by French antislavery groups. The caption reads "I am your equal. Color is nothing; the heart is all. Am I not your brother?" This poster was circulated by *Les Amis des Noirs*, or The Friends of the Blacks. Abbé Raynal belonged to this organization.

For the people of St. Domingue, the major question was: Did the Declaration of the Rights of Man and the Citizen apply to mulattoes and blacks? As yet, this was not explicitly spelled out. But when news of the declaration spread to St. Domingue, it heightened tensions among the different groups in the society. The grands blancs, who had shared in the privileges of the aristocracy, regarded the Revolution with mistrust and fear. The petit blancs were at first enthusiastic at the thought that they would now be equal to the richer whites in St. Domingue. In the streets, petits blancs wore hats with red cockades, or ornaments, like those worn by the Revolution's supporters in Paris.

However, when news came of the declaration, the petit blancs began to have second thoughts. Mulattoes now demanded the end of all legal restrictions on them. If they were successful, the poorer whites would sink below the prosperous mulattoes in the island's society. Furthermore, the mulattoes' demands aroused the whites' deepest fear — that the Declaration of the Rights of Man and the Citizen would free the slaves. Most whites were united in wanting slavery to continue. So when the whites of St. Domingue set up their own colonial assembly, they excluded the mulattoes.

Vincent Ogé, a St. Domingue mulatto living in France, returns to the island bearing the flag of the Revolution. In 1790, the French revolutionary government granted equal rights to mulattoes, but the island authorites refused to recognize the decree. Ogé then led a mulatto rebellion that was quickly crushed by white colonial forces. He was publicly tortured and executed in February 1791.

The mulattoes sent a delegation to the National Assembly in Paris, and in March 1790, the Assembly granted voting rights to all people in St. Domingue who owned property or paid taxes. This clearly included the mulattoes—but not the slaves.

Vincent Ogé, a mulatto who lived in France, returned to St. Domingue. He asked the royal governor of the island to carry out the Assembly's decree. When he refused, Ogé raised a band of armed men and marched toward Le Cap.

Ogé's rebellion was doomed to failure. There were too many whites against too few mulattoes. When Ogé's men were overcome in February 1791, the colonial assembly hanged 22 of them. Ogé and another mulatto leader were punished more cruelly, as a lesson to the mulattoes. In the public square of Le Cap, their arms, legs, and ribs were broken. Then they were tied to wheels and left to face the sun. When they finally died of thirst and pain, their heads were cut off and set up on stakes.

The whites of St. Domingue had given clear notice of the way they would treat anyone who challenged their privileges as a ruling class. But they had earned the bitterness of the mulattoes and in so doing had lost an important group of potential allies that they would need for the next stage of the revolution in St. Domingue.

The Revolution in France and Ogé's rebellion now inspired a slave uprising, one that would be far more successful than the abortive rebellion led by Mackandal more than 30 years before. Boukman, a slave on a plantation in the northern part of St. Domingue, began to meet nightly with other slaves. Like Mackandal, Boukman was a bokor, and he used the Voodoo network to attract more than 10,000 slaves to his cause. Voodoo ceremonies had long been a place where blacks could express their resentment against the whites who enslaved them, and as C. L. R. James noted, many Voodoo rituals included this song:

> Eh! Eh! Bomba! Heu! Heu!
> Canga, bafio té!
> Canga, mouné de lé!
> Cango, do ki la!
> Canga, li!
> ["We swear to destroy the whites and all that they possess; let us die rather than fail to keep this vow."]

In coordinating the uprising, Boukman gathered the leaders of the slaves from various plantations together, and at a solemn ceremony he slit the throat of a pig; each man present drank its blood. Then he chanted these words: "Hearken unto Liberty, that speaks now in all our hearts."

On the night of August 22, 1791, the slaves rose up against their masters. Armed with scythes and machetes, they slaughtered white families in their beds and set fire to anything that would burn — houses, stables, and even the crops. Their ferocity knew no bounds. One group was led by a man who had a white baby impaled on a staff. As flames from the burning plantations lit up the sky, whites who managed to escape fled toward the main northern city of Le Cap.

Black slaves massacre their white masters at the start of the St. Domingue slave uprising on August 22, 1791. Thousands of people were killed in the massacres and reprisals, which engulfed the entire northern half of the colony. Within a few weeks, the blacks controlled the countryside, while the whites held a few cities and towns.

Breda, the plantation where Toussaint lived, was in the path of the rebellion. The plantation manager was away, leaving his wife and two daughters alone. Toussaint protected them, but he soon saw that he could not stem the desire for freedom and revenge among the plantation's 1,000 slaves. In gratitude to the white family that had helped him, he arranged for their safe passage to Le Cap, where they would board a ship and head for the United States. Toussaint took precautions to protect his own family as well, sending his wife and children to Spanish Santo Domingo. Then he rode off to the rebels' camp, leading the slaves of Breda with him.

At this critical moment, Toussaint was about 47 years old, already an advanced age for a slave. But his knowledge of the world was probably greater than that of any other slave on the island. He later described his feelings about the black rebellion: "Those first moments were one of a beautiful delirium, born of a great love of freedom."

Toussaint at first served the rebels as a healer for the wounded. There were many of them. Armed soldiers had gone into the countryside to put down the rebellion. Though the whites used rifles against slaves, who had nothing but farm tools, the slaves swept forward in human waves without concern for their lives. When the soldiers paused to reload their single-shot guns, the slaves swarmed over them.

In a month's time, Boukman's rebels captured and burned several small towns in the countryside. Le Cap, which now sheltered thousands of white refugees, prepared to defend itself against the oncoming blacks.

Boukman had promised the slaves that if they died, they would awake in Africa, a common Voodoo belief. When they reached the defenses of Le Cap, the blacks, fearless in light of the promise of paradise, charged the cannons, thrusting their arms into the barrels. Wave after wave of people charged forward, free at last to take revenge for every lash that the overseers had raked across their back.

But the superior firepower of the defenders saved the town. After a day of bloody fighting, the blacks retreated. At least 10,000 of them lay dead. Sometime during the fighting, Boukman had been killed. His head was cut off and displayed in the public square.

The loss of Boukman was a devastating blow to the blacks, but they still held large areas of the countryside in the northern province. Just a few weeks had passed since the uprising began, but the blacks had already burned some 1,400 plantations to the ground and pushed the whites and their forces into a handful of cities and towns. For now, the blacks were safe from counterattack.

Two black leaders rose to command the slave army. Their names were Jean François and Biassou. They set up camp on one of the captured plantations. Toussaint was there, moving among the wounded, treating them with his healing herbs. Soon he had a title: Chief Physician to the Army.

Toussaint used his knowledge of European military campaigns to give advice to the leaders. He told them that their fight would be a long one. The most

If the National Assembly has the misfortune to legislate on the mulatto status, all is over. The colonists will believe themselves betrayed; the mulattos, instigated by their friends, will go to the last extremity. And the slaves, who possess the same friends and the same means of action, will seek to obtain the same results.
—MOREAU DE SAINT-MERY representative of Martinique in the National Assembly, supporting the colonial viewpoint in his book *Considerations*, published in March 1791

Biassou, one of the first generals to lead the army of black slaves in the revolt against the whites. Toussaint joined the black forces soon after the start of the revolt, serving at first as the chief physician of the army.

immediate need was for food. Having burned the plantations' crops behind them, they had to live on whatever wild plants and animals they could find. Toussaint realized that the ragtag army needed discipline. They must build carefully and avoid destroying what they most needed in their wild forays against plantations.

Before long, Toussaint was put in command of part of the rebel army. He drilled his men the way he had read an army should be trained. He appointed some as officers and showed them how to direct their men in an attack. In only a few months, the white military commanders saw a difference in the way the blacks attacked camps and towns. They no longer charged forward without regard for their own safety; astonishingly, they seemed to have been drilled and trained like European troops.

One day, the French governor in Le Cap received a letter from the rebels. In flowing French phrases, the letter declared the rebels' loyalty to the king (who was, at this time, still the ruler of France). It declared the rebels' desire for peace — but it demanded that all the whites must leave Le Cap and return to their plantations. "We only seek . . . that so precious thing, beloved liberty."

The letter was signed by "the generals and chiefs who make up our army." The French governor assumed from the letter's style that a white Frenchman must be in command of the army. He did not yet know of Toussaint.

The black uprising had so far been confined to the north. In the southern part of the country, however, a new mulatto uprising began. In many towns, fighting broke out between mulattoes and petits blancs.

On November 29, 1791, three commissioners appointed by the National Assembly arrived from France to open negotiations with Jean François and Biassou. Despite its victories, the blacks' army was in dire trouble, suffering from starvation and lack of supplies. Jean François and Biassou believed the commissioners' claim that France would soon send troops to put down the revolt. Thinking their army would be no match for regular French troops, the black leaders offered new peace terms: In exchange for the king's pardon for all who had taken part in the rebellion, the slaves would return to the plantations, with assurances that they would no longer be whipped and that they would have an extra day off besides Sunday.

The terms offered by the black leaders were astonishing; all they were asking for was that a slightly milder form of slavery be instituted. Indeed, it is doubtful that the black leaders could have convinced their followers to return to the life of a slave.

Toussaint was among the black leaders who took part in the negotiations, and one can only speculate as to the reasons why he appeared ready to abandon the cause of freedom. Throughout his career, he tried to avoid bloodshed whenever possible, and he may have been pessimistic about the blacks' chances of overcoming the French army that was on its way.

In any case, the whites' colonial assembly inter-

In St. Domingue everything takes on an air of opulence that dazzles Europeans. That throng of slaves who await the orders and even the lifted finger of a lone individual, confers grandeur on him who commands them. To have four times as many servants as one needs marks the grandiloquence of a wealthy man.
—MOREAU DE SAINT-MERY
representative of Martinique in the National Assembly

vened. The colonists declared they would not accept any agreement made between the commissioners and the slaves. That put a stop to the negotiations, and the commissioners returned to France.

Returning to the rebel camp, Toussaint looked to Spain for help. The Spanish still controlled the eastern half of the island, called Santo Domingo, and they agreed to send Toussaint food and arms. The Spanish, slaveholders themselves, did not act out of generosity; they saw a chance to take back the entire island after the blacks had done the work of driving out the French.

With Spanish help, Toussaint continued training his troops throughout most of 1792. Meanwhile, in the fall of that year, three new commissioners arrived from France. One of them was Léger Sonthonax, an ardent revolutionary. He took over control of the colony, using the 6,000 armed French soldiers he had brought to enforce his authority.

The French troops, commanded by the Comte Étienne-Maynard de Laveaux, were tougher and bet-

Three commissioners sent to St. Domingue by France's king Louis XVI negotiate with black rebels. The rebels, including Toussaint, offered to return to the plantation as slaves in exchange for less severe treatment and the king's pardon, but the offer was refused by the white colonial government.

ter trained than the Creole soldiers who had been unable to subdue the blacks. The French soldiers defeated Toussaint's men in the first battle between the two armies, and Toussaint was wounded. He retreated and reorganized his forces.

A few days later, his arm in a sling, he led his troops against Laveaux once more. The attack failed, and more than half of Toussaint's men were killed. Biassou and Jean François suffered similar defeats in other places, and the black rebellion seemed doomed. Then, as it had before, the French Revolution took a new turn that would completely alter the situation in St. Domingue. The news arrived from France that the king had been executed. France was a republic.

Now the kingdoms of Spain and England were openly at war with the Republic of France. Both countries threatened to send forces to try to take St. Domingue. Laveaux broke off his fight against the slaves and moved his men to the coast to protect the ports against foreign fleets. Toussaint now of-

ficially joined the Spanish side, becoming a colonel in the Spanish army.

In early 1793, a second military force arrived from France, led by General Thomas-François Galbaud. Galbaud had originally been sent to help defeat the slave rebellion, but the execution of the king, which occurred while Galbaud and his troops were at sea, changed his plans; now his mission was to keep St. Domingue in the hands of the monarchists. Many whites in St. Domingue welcomed Galbaud as a savior who would free them from the republican government of France.

Galbaud swiftly took over Le Cap and rooted out all republican resistance. Sonthonax, loyal to the Republic, fled the city. Desperate for help, he offered freedom to any black who would fight on the side of the Republic. He also counted on the support of the mulattoes, who were grateful to the republicans for giving them equal rights with whites.

Sonthonax returned to Le Cap with a large force of blacks and mulattoes and took the city. The victors looted the houses and stores, and two-thirds of the buildings were burned to the ground. General Galbaud and his men were forced to jump into the sea and swim for their lives. Their ships offshore also took on board some 10,000 of the richest white families in St. Domingue. In republican France they would have been considered criminals for having exploited the poor, so many of the wealthy refugees went to the United States, never to return.

On August 29, 1793, Sonthonax kept his promise and declared that all the slaves were free. He expected that they would now rally to the support of the new French government, and many did. But Toussaint knew that Sonthonax's order did not have the official approval of the French government. He still distrusted Sonthonax, fearing that the freedom of the slaves was a temporary measure.

So Toussaint took the remnants of his force — about 600 men — across the border into Santo Domingo, where his family waited. The Spanish gave him the official rank of colonel in their army. Biassou and Jean François, who also went over to the Spanish, were named generals.

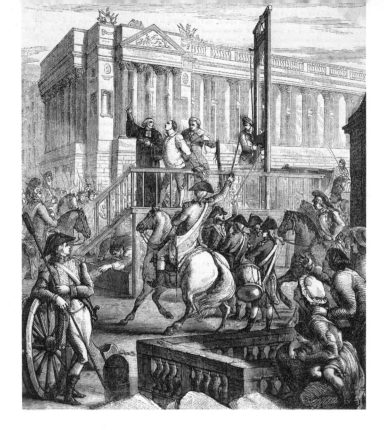

The execution of King Louis XVI in Paris on January 21, 1793, made France the first republic in Europe and prompted most European nations to declare war against France. French troops in St. Domingue, who were on the verge of putting down the black revolt, broke off fighting to prepare against attack by British and Spanish forces.

From Santo Domingo, Toussaint sent a message to his fellow blacks in St. Domingue, giving himself a greater title:

> Brothers and Friends
> I am Toussaint L'Ouverture. My name is perhaps known to you. I have undertaken vengeance. I want Liberty and Equality to reign in Saint Domingue. I work to bring them into existence. Brothers, unite with us and fight by our side for the same cause.
>
> Toussaint L'Ouverture,
> General of the Army of the
> King for the Public Good

It was the first time he signed himself by the name he is known in history. *L'ouverture* means "the opening." Some say that white Creole leaders had dubbed him that because he always found an opening through which to attack. Toussaint himself later told the Comte de Laveaux, "I thought it was a good name for bravery." Whatever the reason, he now declared himself the leader of the black revolution. He would not falter until his goals of liberty and equality had been won.

4

Citizen Toussaint

Toussaint knew that the Spanish were using him and the blacks of St. Domingue for their own purposes, but he in turn was using the Spanish. Toussaint did not trust Sonthonax, the representative of a French republican government that had not yet abolished slavery.

Moreover, Toussaint had his own ambition — to lead the former slaves himself. "Having been the first to champion your cause," he proclaimed, "it is my duty to continue to labor for it. I cannot permit another to rob me of the initiative. Since I have begun, I will know how to conclude. Join me and you will enjoy the rights of freemen sooner than any other way."

Toussaint used Spanish help to get better weapons and train his troops. He surrounded himself with an officer corps of high talent. Jean-Jacques Dessalines, who would one day rule Haiti, often served as his second-in-command. Around 40 years old at the time of the slave rebellion, Dessalines bore on his back the scars of the whip of a cruel black

If Toussaint and his blacks should succumb easily to their fate, the wave of French empire would roll on to Louisiana and sweep far up the Mississippi.
—HENRY ADAMS
American historian

A hand-painted button from Toussaint's uniform illustrates a rural scene on St. Domingue. By 1794, Toussaint had emerged as the leading general in the bloody fight for control of the colony.

overseer. Unable to read or write, he only learned to sign his name near the end of his life. Known as the Tiger, his fearlessness and brutality struck fear in the hearts of his foes, but he himself remained in awe of Toussaint.

Other commanders included Jacques Maurepas and Toussaint's nephew Moise. Maurepas came from an old free black family and was a man of culture. The dashing Moise, fond of women, was the most popular soldier in the army. Born in Africa, he had crossed the Atlantic as a child in a slave ship. In addition, two of Toussaint's younger brothers, Paul and Jean-Pierre, served with distinction.

With Spanish help, Toussaint led his forces back across the border into St. Domingue. They swept over the northern part of the island, taking town after town — but without burning or looting; Toussaint had instilled discipline in his men. The restraint of the new black army won over many whites and mulattoes; even some French officers, unhappy with the new French government, deserted their posts and swelled the ranks of Toussaint's army. By the end of 1793, Toussaint and the Spanish had moved into the center of the country, driving a wedge between the French-controlled areas in the north and south.

In the south, another foreign force had entered the fray. The white planters had turned to the British, whose king they preferred to the French revolutionary government. The British saw a chance to seize the rich colony and landed troops at the town of Jérémie on the southern coast in September 1793. Using their naval supremacy, the British blockaded the coast, preventing supplies from getting through to the French troops.

The British moved toward Port-au-Prince, the chief city of the south. Leaving Laveaux in command in the north, Sonthonax, too, headed for Port-au-Prince, to direct the city's defense against the British advance.

Faced with attack on two fronts, the French were in a desperate position. "We have been reduced to six ounces of bread a day," Laveaux reported. "If we had powder we would rest easier. We have no shoes,

It was remarkable to see these Africans with bare torsos and equipped only with cartridge pouch, sword and musket, give an example of perfect self-control. . . . They trembled before their officers and were respected by the people. To have succeeded in disciplining these barbarians was Toussaint's supreme triumph.

—PAMPHILE DE LACROIX
opponent of Toussaint's
units and later historian of
the revolution in
St. Domingue

48

shirts, clothes, soap or tobacco. Our soldiers mount guard barefooted. We have not even a flint to issue." Laveaux, fearing he could not hold the north against the black and Spanish forces, had no choice but to negotiate with Toussaint.

Meanwhile in France, the Revolution had entered its most radical phase. In an emotional meeting of the national legislature in February 1794, the delegates issued a historic proclamation:

> The National Convention [the new name for the National Assembly] declares slavery abolished in all the colonies. In consequence it declares that all men, without distinction of color, [living] in the colonies, are French citizens, and enjoy all the rights assured under the Constitution.

The resolution was unanimously adopted, and suddenly the French republican government had allied itself with the former slaves. When word of this development reached Toussaint, he sent representatives to Laveaux and proposed a secret agreement to change sides. A relieved Laveaux gladly agreed. Now Toussaint was in a position to turn against his erstwhile Spanish allies.

The governor of Spanish Santo Domingo, Don García, had been warned by Biassou that Toussaint was planning treachery, and Don García imprisoned Moise and Toussaint's wife to forestall such

Toussaint accepts the surrender of French generals. By late 1793, Toussaint and his Spanish allies had established control over much of central St. Domingue; meanwhile, invading British forces gained a foothold in the southern portion of the colony.

Jean-Jacques Dessalines, who often served as Toussaint's second-in-command. A former slave whose hatred for the whites made him a ferocious fighter, Dessalines would eventually be the man to declare the colony's independence; in today's Haiti his memory is more highly venerated than that of Toussaint.

an action. But Toussaint persuaded Don García to release them, promising that he would shortly return to battle. This was true enough, but Toussaint did not tell him on what side he intended to fight.

Sending his wife and children back to St. Domingue, Toussaint attacked the Spanish garrison after Sunday mass. Quickly overcoming them, Toussaint marched on Biassou's camp, where some of his officers were held. Toussaint's brother Jean-Pierre was killed in the fighting, but Toussaint destroyed the camp. Biassou fled, leaving behind his carriage, a gold watch, and a diamond-encrusted snuff box. Toussaint, ever the gentleman, ordered them returned to Biassou. Soon after, Toussaint defeated Jean-François as well.

When Toussaint met Laveaux face to face in July 1794, Laveaux wore a hat with red feathers — the color of the revolution. Toussaint's hat had white feathers, showing his loyalty to the late king Louis. Laveaux took one of the feathers from his hat and placed it on Toussaint's. He addressed the former slave as "Citizen Toussaint"; *citizen* was the title the French Revolution gave to all people of France, to do away with the old titles that separated nobles from peasants.

Toussaint seldom trusted anyone, but he found a kindred spirit in the former French nobleman, Laveaux. Laveaux became one of Toussaint's greatest admirers, and the men frequently exchanged letters and gifts. In a war where so many people changed sides frequently, their friendship would last through the hard times that lay ahead. Laveaux's support would give Toussaint the final push he needed to take full control of St. Domingue.

For the time being, Sonthonax was out of the way. He and the other commissioners were recalled to France to answer charges of treason, which had been laid by some of the white Creoles who had fled there. Sonthonax faced a trial and perhaps the guillotine. Laveaux was left in control of those parts of the colony that remained loyal to France.

Seeing Toussaint's ability, Laveaux made him a major general in the French republican army. Among the troops in his new command was a former slave named Henri Christophe. Born on the nearby British-controlled island of Grenada but raised in St. Domingue, Christophe had seen more wars than most. When his French master volunteered to join the colonists in the American Revolution, he took Christophe with him; later, Christophe had served with the French forces that put down Ogé's mulatto rebellion. Christophe become one of Toussaint's closest aides.

Laveaux put Toussaint in charge of the northern part of St. Domingue. With the countryside devastated by the fighting, Toussaint wanted blacks to return to the plantations to grow food for the colony and to rebuild the economy that was based on plantation labor. At the same time, he was occupied with driving out the remaining Spanish troops from the north.

Those who served with him remembered that the 50-year-old Toussaint, whom they called the Old Man, could ride farther and faster than anyone else. He seemed tireless; when he dismounted, he began dictating letters to his secretaries and kept them

After God, it was Laveaux.
—TOUSSAINT L'OUVERTURE
on the French general, one
of the few men he trusted

awake far into the night. Toussaint got by with as few as two hours' sleep daily.

When he had secured the north, Toussaint marched against the British in the south. In his first battle, a regiment of his mulattoes went over to the British side. "I have treated them like a father," Toussaint wrote to Lavaeux, "and they have repaid me with this dastardly attempt to betray me to the enemy." This incident hardened Toussaint's attitude against the mulattoes. In the future, he would trust them only when circumstances forced him to.

In the midst of the British campaign, Toussaint had to return to the north to put down a rebellion of blacks. The blacks who had returned to the plantations at Toussaint's urging were unhappy. Though they were now called cultivators instead of slaves, they did not feel they were truly free. Indeed, Toussaint ordered strict punishment be imposed upon those blacks who failed to perform long hard duty in the fields. In addition, British agents, often mulattoes, circulated among the cultivators, telling them that Toussaint wanted to make them slaves again.

Toussaint met with a group of the cultivators. One by one they poured out their complaints to him. They wanted their own small plots of land. Most of the food they grew on the plantations was taken from them. They did not understand why they should grow food for others. They wondered why they had not received the profits that had been promised them.

Toussaint believed that the colony needed a more efficient agriculture than the small plots the cultivators wanted. Appealing to the awe and gratitude the cultivators felt toward him Toussaint issued a proclamation: "O You Africans, my brothers, you who have cost me so many battles, so much labor and so much concern, you whose liberty was created with your own blood. How long will I have the shame of seeing my deluded children turn from the advice of a father who loves them?"

Toussaint rallied the cultivators by using the slogan of the French Revolution: Liberty, Equality,

I am Toussaint L'Ouverture. My name is perhaps known to you. I have undertaken to avenge you. I want liberty and equality to reign in St. Domingue.
—TOUSSAINT L'OUVERTURE
proclamation of
August 29, 1793

Fraternity. These words were as meaningful to former slaves as to French peasants. Telling them that "Liberty cannot exist without work," Toussaint persuaded the blacks to return to the plantations.

He turned his attention again to fighting the British in the south. Temporarily laying aside his distrust of the mulattoes, Toussaint accepted the support of some mulatto forces under the command of André Rigaud and Louis-Jacques Beauvais, who had been harassing the British. On February 2, 1795, the night before a combined black-mulatto attack against the British was to begin, Toussaint told his troops: "Show yourselves to be men who know what liberty means and are prepared to defend

Henri Christophe, another of Toussaint's top military commanders. Like Dessalines a former slave, Christophe would later rule an independent Haiti.

CARIBBEAN SEA

HISPANIOLA

Môle St. Nicholas

Cap François

Limbé

Gonaïves

ST. DOMINGUE (French)

SANTO DOMINGO (Spanish)

Jérémie

Port-au-Prince

Mirebalais

Santo Domingo

Petit-Goâve

Jacmel

Hispaniola at the time of the Haitian Revolution; today the island is divided into Haiti in the west and the Dominican Republic in the east.

it." The following day he won the first of seven battles in seven days.

Among those fighting on the British side were French nobles who had fled France to escape the Revolution; they were called emigrés. Toussaint surrounded a fort containing 800 emigrés under the command of the Marquis d'Espinville and offered to enter the fort to negotiate personally with d'Espinville. The marquis received him dressed in the elegant uniform of a royal French officer. Toussaint wore his customary battle dress: a cotton bandana wrapped around his head, a sword at his waist, and an old suit, the legs of which were stained with the sweat of his horse.

The marquis announced that he and his men would fight to the death rather than be dishonored by surrendering and being slaughtered. Toussaint assured him that the marquis's men, if taken prisoner, would be well treated. Any who wished to join Toussaint's army could do so. The marquis replied that he could hardly accept the word of a rebellious slave. Toussaint put his hand on the hilt of his sword, in the manner of a French officer, and said, "I swear it by my sword." D'Espinville then accepted the offer, and Toussaint kept his promise.

On another occasion, a white officer in his force deserted to the British. In a later battle, the deserter was captured by Toussaint's men and brought before him. Tousssaint merely smiled and said, "I see that we are too good friends for fate to keep us long apart." He allowed the man to resume his former position of command.

Toussaint was also generous to the white plantation owners in the south, allowing them to take their belongings — which in some cases included gold that he needed badly — and flee to Port-au-Prince, by now a British stronghold. His fight was with soldiers, not civilians, and he wanted the support of whites to rebuild St. Domingue once peace was restored. Toussaint was performing a balancing act; he had to stay on as good terms as possible with all the various racial and social groups of St. Domingue, who had long nursed a virulent hatred for each other.

By the end of 1795, the British had been driven back into a few important coastal cities, although their forces would remain on the island for three more years. Spain, however, had been defeated in Europe by the French and ceased to be a threat in St. Domingue. A peace treaty was signed between the countries in September 1795, in which the Spanish ceded Santo Domingo to France.

Biassou and Jean-François, who were still leading black troops on the Spanish side, left the island. Biassou went to Florida, then a Spanish possession, where he died in a brawl. Jean-François enjoyed the rest of his life as a wealthy nobleman in Spain.

Victory over the foreign foes seemed near, but within St. Domingue, tensions between the various racial and social groups increased. The mulattoes, fearing Toussaint's growing power and his close relationship with Laveaux, the white republican governor of the colony, threatened to set up an independent government in the south under Rigaud. Toussaint wrote Laveaux that many of the mulatto landowners in the area he controlled were

It is true, General, that I had been deceived by the enemies of the republic; but what man can pride himself on avoiding all the traps of wickedness?
—TOUSSAINT L'OUVERTURE
letter to General Laveaux,
May 18, 1794

pro-British. He said that they "have sworn to do away with me. . . . I am to perish in some ambush. . . . Let them trap me well, for if they miss me I will not spare them."

The mulattoes struck first, but in the north at Le Cap. On the morning of March 20, 1796, Laveaux was dragged from his bed by men sent by Villate, the mulatto military commander of the city. Barefoot and in his nightshirt, Laveaux was thrown in jail. Villate proclaimed himself the new governor of St. Domingue.

Toussaint sent Henri Christophe to Le Cap with a force of troops. To protect against other mulattoes rising in support of Villate, Toussaint remained behind. Villate fled when Christophe's force reached the city, and Laveaux was freed. Toussaint arrived shortly afterward, entering Le Cap with 90 dragoons. When he sent representatives to negotiate with Villate, Villate declared that he would negotiate only with Toussaint. But Toussaint refused, fearing treachery if he went to Villate's camp.

Villate still hoped to undercut Toussaint's power. He told Toussaint's representatives that Laveaux had a storehouse full of chains that were to be used to re-enslave the blacks. The rumor spread through Le Cap, and a crowd gathered at Laveaux's house, calling for his death. Toussaint arrived, led the crowd to the government warehouse, and opened its doors, letting everyone see that there were no chains inside.

At the head of his cavalry and infantry, Toussaint appeared with Laveaux in the public square of Le Cap. Toussaint listened as Laveaux described him as "that black Spartacus foreseen by Raynal whose destiny is to avenge the outrages of his race." He received from Laveaux the position of lieutenant governor of St. Domingue. "After God, Laveaux," Toussaint graciously replied.

Tousssaint's life was complicated by the return to St. Domingue of Sonthonax, once again a commissioner. By the time Sonthonax had arrived in France to face charges of treason, the French government had changed, and he was cleared. His new orders as part of a five-member commission were to restore order in the colony.

Although Sonthonax was popular with the blacks, who remembered him as a liberator, the mulattoes distrusted him. Instead of following a policy of reconciliation with the mulattoes as Laveaux had intended, Sonthonax struck out at them. He arrested and deported Villate. Then he sent a commission to the south with orders to investigate Rigaud's involvement in the plot to overthrow Laveaux. Though they found no evidence, they treated Rigaud roughly.

Toussaint and his aides interrogate a British spy. After the French revolutionary government abolished slavery in February 1794, Toussaint and the other blacks allied with France and turned against the Spanish and British.

Whites massacre blacks during the war in St. Domingue. Such mass killings of members of one racial group by another were a constant feature of the long Haitian Revolution. On several occasions, Toussaint ordered his black forces to massacre mulattoes and whites.

This was particularly unwise since Rigaud's army controlled parts of the southern portion of the colony. Toussaint needed Rigaud and felt that the only way to ensure his support was to get rid of the hot-tempered and impulsive Sonthonax. He began a delicate diplomatic game, showing once again how subtle he could be at maneuvering others according to his designs.

St. Domingue had the right to elect deputies to the legislature in France. Toussaint proposed both Laveaux and Sonthonax for the posts and used his influence to get them elected. To Laveaux, exhausted by his years in the colony, this was a relief. He wanted to return home to his family.

But Sonthonax was another matter. Regarding himself as the liberator of the blacks in St. Domingue, he stalled his departure. In December 1796, he called Toussaint to meet with him at Le Cap. According to Toussaint, Sonthonax proposed that all the remaining whites on the island should be killed, and St. Domingue would become a republic independent from France. Toussaint's reply was, "Well, Commissioner, when I have declared my independence of France and have massacred all the whites, what do you propose I should do with *you*?"

Toussaint wrote a letter to the French government, telling them of Sonthonax's proposal. When Sonthonax heard of this, he began to plot against Toussaint, increasing the pay of troops under his command while cutting off supplies intended for Toussaint's men.

Toussaint led a large force to the outskirts of Le Cap in a show of strength designed to inform Sonthonax that it was time for him to go back to France. Sonthonax had no choice but to comply; he and his family headed for the harbor, where a ship was readying to sail for France. Blacks lined the streets of the city to pay their respects to the white man who had played an important role in freeing the slaves.

With the departure of Sonthonax, Toussaint's power increased. But the future was nevertheless uncertain. In the south, Toussaint could not count on Rigaud's loyalty, and there was always the threat that Sonthonax would make trouble for him with the French government. To show his loyalty to the mother country, Toussaint decided to send his two young sons, Placide and Isaac, to France to be educated.

The boys embraced their parents in farewell. Toussaint told them that they would learn to be gentlemen before their return. Their mother, knowing that she would not see Placide and Isaac for years, wept. But there would be some benefit to their stay in France besides the education they would acquire: They would not be in St. Domingue for the terrible bloodletting that was soon to occur.

5

The War of the Knives

Now that Sonthonax and Laveaux were gone, Toussaint officially ruled St. Domingue. As lieutenant governor and commander of the army, he would hold the reins of power until France sent a new governor.

Ironically, the first orders to come from France called Sonthonax back home, something Toussaint had already taken care of. His recall, as before, was prompted by French planters who complained bitterly to the French government about Sonthonax's policies. They wanted to restore St. Domingue to what they believed was its former glory. The idea of a former black slave in charge was anathema to them.

Toussaint kept himself informed about the political situation in France. He realized that the current French government, called the Directory, was more conservative than the earlier revolutionary governments. Some members of the Directory sympathized with the French planters. There was discussion of restoring slavery.

One can reproach the inhabitants of St. Domingue, including the blacks, for many faults, even terrible crimes. But even in France, where the limits of sociability are clearly drawn, doesn't one see its inhabitants, in the struggle between despotism and liberty, going to all the excesses for which the blacks are reproached by their enemies?
—TOUSSAINT L'OUVERTURE
excerpt from letter
to the Directory,
October 28, 1797

A contemporary Spanish depiction of Toussaint, who in 1797 was appointed commander in chief of French forces in St. Domingue. Having already driven Spanish forces from the colony, Toussaint's immediate concern was preventing the restoration of slavery by white reactionaries.

General Thomas Maitland, commander of the British forces in St. Domingue. Unable to overcome Toussaint's army, he negotiated a settlement with the black general that allowed some British troops to remain in the south. Toussaint, however, declined his invitation to join the British against the French.

At the end of 1797, Toussaint sent a letter to the French government. He affirmed his loyalty to France, but in eloquent words warned against any attempt to restore slavery. "Do you think," Toussaint asked,

> that men who have been able to enjoy the blessing of liberty will calmly see it snatched away? [The blacks of St. Domingue endured] their chains only so long as they did not know any condition of life more happy than that of slavery. But today when they have left it, if they had a thousand lives they would sacrifice them all rather than be forced into slavery again.

The French government did not yet have plans to restore slavery, but it wanted to curtail Toussaint's power. The Directory sent a new commissioner,

Théodore Hédouville, to St. Domingue. Before leaving France, Hédouville heard Laveaux shower praise on Toussaint and Sonthonax roundly condemn him. Hédouville decided to stop at the eastern end of the island to speak with Philip Roume, the French commissioner at the former Spanish colony of Santo Domingo. Roume called Toussaint "a philosopher, a legislator, a general, and a good citizen."

Hédouville met Toussaint in the spring of 1798. The Frenchman flattered Toussaint in lavish terms, showing already that he misunderstood his character. Toussaint was not impressed, but he realized that he had to keep Hédouville from causing trouble. French representatives were by this time old hat for Toussaint.

Toussaint left the conference to resume his campaign against the British. Though there was no danger of them taking over the island, they had continued to be a thorn in his side. British forces still held some coastal cities and the British naval blockade was stifling the island's trade.

The main British land force was now bottled up in Port-au-Prince. The new commander, General Thomas Maitland, faced an impossible military situation. Yellow fever, a disease to which those who lived on the island were immune, was decimating British troops. High casualties, high costs, and lack of success had made the military adventure unpopular in Britain. Maitland decided to try to strike a deal with Toussaint.

In April 1798, negotiations began between representatives of the two men. The British agreed to leave Port-au-Prince and the surrounding area, leaving all military installations intact. In return, Toussaint agreed to spare the lives and property of the civilians who remained, many of whom were emigrés from France who looked to the British to protect them. After the British withdrawal, Toussaint entered Port-au-Prince in triumph to cries of "Vive le Libérateur!"

Back in Le Cap, Hédouville was piqued by Toussaint's negotiating with the British and tried to assert his authority. He criticized the terms Toussaint had accepted, especially his agreeing to protect the

> *I tell you it would be to attempt the impossible: we have known how to face dangers to obtain our liberty, we shall know how to face death to maintain it.*
> —TOUSSAINT L'OUVERTURE
> letter warning the Directory against any thoughts of restoring slavery, November 5, 1797

emigrés in British-held territory. By revolutionary French law, emigrés were liable to lose their property. Hédouville declared that the emigrés would be expelled from the colony and their land confiscated. Toussaint, in response, offered his resignation. Hédouville could not afford this and was forced to withdraw his order. But he plotted to undercut Toussaint's power.

The British now held only the towns of Jérémie in the south and Môle St. Nicholas on the northwest coast. Maitland still hoped to keep a foothold in the south, and his forces suddenly broke out of Jérémie, attacking the troops of Rigaud, Toussaint's unsteady mulatto ally. If Maitland hoped Toussaint would not help Rigaud, he was wrong. Toussaint moved reinforcements south and the British were thrown back.

Maitland decided on a complete withdrawal. He met with Toussaint at the end of August to discuss the surrender terms. The British general surprised Toussaint by offering to end the naval blockade. He slyly suggested that Toussaint should declare the island independent and make himself ruler. If he did, he could expect Britain's navy to keep the French from coming to oust him. Toussaint, as he had before to Sonthonax, turned down the offer. He believed St. Domingue still needed help from France.

Maitland held a grand dinner in Toussaint's honor. When Toussaint entered Maitland's headquarters, British troops passed in review before him and fired their guns in salute. At the table, Toussaint commented pointedly that France had never shown him as much honor as did Britain.

Word of this reached Hédouville, and the Frenchman summoned both Toussaint and Rigaud to meet with him in Le Cap. Toussaint offered to share a carriage with Rigaud for the two-day trip. He knew that if he could persuade Rigaud to support him, their united force could stand firm against any opponent.

But Rigaud resented Toussaint's popularity with both whites and blacks and the honors Laveaux had given him by naming him commander of the army.

I feel that although I am a Negro, though I have not received as fine an education as you and the officers of his Britannic Majesty, I feel that if I were to be guilty of such infamy it would reflect upon the honour of my country and I would have tarnished its glory.
—TOUSSAINT L'OUVERTURE
to the British general White
on his ordering the deaths
of the captured soldiers of
Toussaint's army

Rigaud could not overcome his prejudice toward the blacks nor his hatred for the whites. As a child, Rigaud had been sent to France for an education. When France had sent soldiers to fight on the side of the American colonists in the American Revolution, he had volunteered. On his return to St. Domingue, Rigaud had become a goldsmith and prospered. But his services to France, his education, and his wealth had never earned him the right to sit at the table of a white man. He would not be satisfied until the whites were humbled and mulattoes ruled St. Domingue.

Toussaint had a different vision of St. Domingue's future: a multiracial society, something that was unheard of at that time. Though he was proud of being black, Toussaint admired French culture and did not hate whites. Though he distrusted mulattoes, he knew that they must play a part in the colony's future. During a public speech, he had lifted two bottles, one containing red wine, the

Théodore Hédouville, the commissioner sent to St. Domingue by the French government in 1798. After Toussaint negotiated a settlement with the remaining British forces in the colony, Hédouville attempted to strip him of his power.

65

John Adams, the second president of the United States. In 1799, Adams signed a three-way treaty aimed at blocking French efforts in St. Domingue with Toussaint and Great Britain. A key element of the pact forbade Toussaint from spreading the slave rebellion to the southern United States.

other, white. He poured the red into the white and showed the crowd that they blended together to make one color.

On the fateful carriage ride to Le Cap, Toussaint relaxed his guard. He tried to make Rigaud see what the colony might become. If the whites could be persuaded to return to St. Domingue, the colony could be self-sufficient.

Rigaud later claimed that Toussaint astonished him with a proposal that they work together to create an independent government. If so, and if Rigaud had agreed, the future history of the island might have been very different. But when the two arrived at Le Cap, Hédouville met with them separately. Rigaud fell for the Frenchman's flattery. Hédouville let him imagine that France would name him the governor of St. Domingue. Rigaud told Hédouville of Toussaint's "plot" to declare the island independent.

Hédouville knew that Toussaint's troops would rise up if he tried to arrest Toussaint on the word of Rigaud. Instead, he tried to stir up trouble between the two, hoping to weaken both. He told Toussaint of Rigaud's accusation and suggested that Toussaint should arrest him. But Toussaint refused to rise to the bait.

Hédouville was not discouraged. He thought Toussaint might be taken in by another offer and proposed that he invade the nearby British colony of Jamaica to free the slaves there. But Toussaint refused; his only concern was St. Domingue. By now, Toussaint knew that Hédouville's presence on the island meant only further trouble.

The French representative then attempted to turn Toussaint's own men against him. Hédouville kept food and supplies from being sent to Moise's forces, which were stationed at Fort Liberté, near Le Cap. When Moise's men tried to take the supplies by force, Hédouville relieved Moise of his command. He ordered Toussaint to go to Fort Liberté; and arrest the "traitorous" Moise.

But Toussaint, instead of attacking his own men, called on the cultivators to leave their plantations and march on Le Cap. He told them Hédouville was planning to restore slavery. As thousands of angry blacks converged on the city, Hédouville and a thousand of his men fled to ships in the harbor and left for France.

Before he left, Hédouville named Rigaud to a rank equal to that of Toussaint and appointed him commander of the southern region of the colony. To the Directory he reported: "The sole hope of checking Toussaint L'Ouverture even for the moment lies in . . . fostering the hate between the mulattoes and blacks, and by opposing Rigaud to Toussaint."

Toussaint demonstrated his loyalty by declaring that the colony would continue to follow the laws and constitution of France. He sent letters to the Directory criticizing Hédouville's unwise actions. And he called Roume from Santo Domingo to be the French governor for St. Domingue.

Roume arrived at the beginning of 1799 and reported to the French government that "Toussaint

L'Ouverture and the other black generals are truly the saviors of St. Domingue and the benefactors of France." Roume was so impressed with Toussaint that he publicly stated that he would not do anything without seeking Toussaint's advice.

Rigaud was bitterly disappointed. Even so, Toussaint once more tried to patch up his differences with the mulatto leader. They met for the last time to discuss a dispute over which of them should control Grand and Petit Goâve, two southern towns that had been occupied by the British. Roume settled the argument in Toussaint's favor and Rigaud stormed out of the meeting.

From February through the middle of June, the two erstwhile allies engaged in a war of words. Each labeled the other a rebel and a traitor to France. Toussaint accused Rigaud of wanting to suppress the blacks. Rigaud protested that he backed the freedom of blacks. But he had referred to them as "cannibals," and in Rigaud's army blacks were never allowed to rise above a captain's rank.

Toussaint prepared for war. Before leaving Port-au-Prince, he gathered the mulattoes in the cathedral and gave a threatening speech:

> Everyone knows that you are seeking mastery over the colony, that you wish to exterminate the whites and enslave the blacks. . . . I see to the bottom of your souls. You are ready to rise against me. But even though my troops [are leaving], I leave here my eye and my arm: my eye to watch, my arm to strike.

Toussaint took other steps to strengthen his position. He persuaded Roume to declare Rigaud in rebellion, and he sent an envoy to the United States government, then headed by President John Adams. Toussaint valued the friendship of the new nation to the north, and he hoped the United States would play a helpful role in the economic reconstruction of St. Domingue.

The United States had its own reasons to regard Toussaint's proposal favorably. At the time, it was involved in an undeclared war with France. French ships based in the Caribbean were capturing American merchant ships bound for Europe to keep them from supplying France's enemy, Britain. Further-

Hédouville is depicted conferring with Toussaint in this contemporary Spanish woodcut. Before the black general expelled him from the colony, Hédouville advised the French government that "the sole hope of checking Toussaint L'Ouverture even for the moment lies in . . . fostering the hate between the mulattoes and blacks."

more, the American consul in St. Domingue admired Toussaint. He reported home on the tensions between Toussaint and Rigaud:

> Both wish to reign, but by different means, and with different views. Rigaud would deluge the country with blood to accomplish this . . . and slaughter indiscriminately whites, blacks, and even the leading chiefs of his own color. . . . Toussaint, on the contrary, [wants to rule] by the united efforts of all the inhabitants, whose friend and protector he wishes to be.

On May 22, 1799, Toussaint signed a three-way treaty with the United States and Great Britain. The two countries agreed not to send supplies to ports on the southern coast of St. Domingue, thus cutting off Rigaud from his sources of supply. In return, Toussaint promised not to allow his forces to be used for attacks by France on the British West Indies nor on the southern United States.

But most important of all, the British and the Americans did not want Toussaint to spread his slave revolution outside St. Domingue. In an amendment to the treaty, the two countries, both of which had extensive slave populations (the United States in its southern states, Britain in its Caribbean colonies), declared their opposition to the introduction of "dangerous principles" among their slaves.

During the treaty negotiations, Toussaint had acted as the head of a sovereign state. Roume, officially the governor, could only watch on the sidelines.

On June 18, 1799, Rigaud's forces attacked Petit and Grand Goâve, which were held by a small garrison of Toussaint's forces. After storming into the towns, Rigaud took no prisoners, slaughtering whites and blacks alike.

The mulattoes' long-stifled hatred now erupted in bloody vengeance, as they rose up in both south and north to attack blacks and whites. The ensuing civil war was fought so viciously that those without guns battled with knives, clubs, nails — any weapon they could find. It was called the War of the Knives, and it forever tore apart the society of St. Domingue.

Sending Moise and Dessalines to fight Rigaud in the south, Toussaint moved to crush mulatto rebellions in the north. Henri Christophe rounded up the mulatto leaders in Le Cap and executed them. This time, there was to be no mercy.

Toussaint's amazing energy enabled him to ride on horseback 65 to 70 miles a day, rallying his followers. The mulattoes laid plans to ambush him. The first bullets killed Toussaint's doctor, who was riding with him. Toussaint's hat was shot off, but he was unhurt. The attackers fled. Toussaint got into a carriage and rode on for a short while. Then he abruptly stopped the carriage and ordered the driver to proceed without him. Toussaint and his men followed at a distance. As the carriage moved

There is no law left in St. Domingue. The will of Toussaint and the other generals' arbitrary whims are the basis for all that is done.
—a French agent reporting to the minister of marine in Paris

around a hill, gunfire again broke out. The carriage driver lost his life, but once more Toussaint escaped.

He captured Port-au-Prince and extracted the vengeance he had promised. Some mulattoes were stuffed into cannons and blown to bits. Toussaint's men rounded up others on boats and rowed them offshore where they were stabbed and thrown into the sea. For days, the tide carried their bodies back onto the beaches.

With his base secured, Toussaint moved to destroy Rigaud's forces in the south. He had an army of 55,000 men to Rigaud's 10,000. But the mulatto forces were well trained and well entrenched in the region they were most familiar with.

The key to victory for Toussaint was Jacmel, a town located on the south coast of the long, narrow peninsula of southern St. Domingue. It guarded the heart of mulatto territory. Toussaint's forces, com-

A massacre at the start of the civil war in mid-1799, when St. Domingue mulattoes struck against blacks and whites alike. Toussaint narrowly escaped death several times during the interracial fighting and ordered the execution of hundreds of mulattoes when his black forces retook Port-au-Prince and the towns of the south.

A portrait by the French artist Jean-Jacques David of the French general Napoleon Bonaparte. In November 1799, Napoleon became dictator of France and ordered an end to the black-mulatto warfare in St. Domingue at about the same time Toussaint completed his victory over mulatto forces. Napoleon confirmed Toussaint as the colony's commander in chief.

manded by Dessalines and Henri Christophe, laid siege to Jacmel in November.

The commander in the town was Alexandre Pétion, and he defended it heroically. Because U.S. warships blockaded the nearby coast, no food or military supplies could get through. Conditions within the town grew desperate. As the food ran out, people ate horses, then dogs and cats, and finally rats, birds, leaves, and grass.

To try to preserve food, Pétion sent the old people and children through the city's gates. He trusted in Toussaint's customary mercy toward his enemies. But Dessalines was a different kind of man. He ordered his troops to mow down the refugees as the city's defenders watched from the walls. Four months into the siege, with all hope fading, Pétion tried to fight his way out of the trap on March 11, 1800. Though Pétion himself escaped, most of his men were killed, along with the remaining residents of Jacmel.

During the siege of Jacmel, Toussaint learned that three new commissioners had been sent from France. Once again, the government there had changed. On November 9, 1799, General Napoleon Bonaparte had overthrown the Directory and named himself first consul of France. The commissioners brought Napoleon's orders: Toussaint was renamed commander in chief of the island's army, but the war with Rigaud had to stop.

Toussaint had heard of Napoleon's ability and his ruthlessness toward his enemies — and he knew that when Napoleon gave an order, he expected it to be carried out. Toussaint made a serious attempt to negotiate peace terms with Rigaud, promising amnesty for the rebels, and ordered his own men to stop their attacks. But Rigaud refused to surrender, even after the fall of Jacmel. As Rigaud's forces fled, he ordered everything in their path put to the torch. But his luck had run out; severe rains put out the fires.

Still, Rigaud gathered his meager forces for a final, futile assault against Dessalines. Rigaud was nearly captured in the attack, but he escaped and fled the island. When he arrived in France and received an audience with Napoleon, he railed against Toussaint. But the first consul was not sympathetic. "General, I have only one fault to find with you—you were not victorious," said Napoleon.

Toussaint, supreme once again in St. Domingue, promised clemency in dealing with the defeated. However, his treatment of the mulattoes showed little of his past generosity and forgiveness. The War of the Knives had left bitterness on all sides, and Toussaint emerged from it a changed man. He himself ordered 300 prisoners of war put to death.

He placed Dessalines in charge of the conquered south, and Dessalines treated the mulattoes with barbaric cruelty. They were publicly tortured, buried alive, and executed by the thousands with the bayonets of his troops. When Toussaint received reports of his aide's ferocious reprisals, his response was mild. "I told him to prune the trees," said Toussaint, "not uproot them."

The only nation toward whom you may be obliged to assume a hostile attitude is the United States, which may be seized with a fit of madness. Two warships and a few frigates will suffice to keep them in check.
—NAPOLEON
instructing General Leclerc

6

"There Is But One Toussaint L'Ouverture"

Toussaint had conquered St. Domingue, but the island was still not free. Though the Spanish had legally ceded Santo Domingo to France, their troops remained on the eastern part of Hispaniola, where slavery was still legal, despite the presence of a French commissioner. Toussaint announced it was time to force the Spanish out.

Roume decided that Toussaint was going too far. At last he attempted to exercise his authority as governor, but to no avail; Toussaint simply arrested him in November 1800. Toussaint boldly wrote to Napoleon that he had been "obliged to invite Citizen Roume to give up his duties and retire . . . until further orders." Toussaint hoped Napoleon would forgive him if he won a victory.

At the beginning of 1801, Toussaint moved his troops across the border. The conquest gave him little trouble, and after a few battles, he was master of the entire island of Hispaniola. The flag of the French republic — the tricolor of blue, white, and red — was raised over Santo Domingo's capital. At the mass celebrating the victory, Toussaint stood in the pulpit of the church and announced the abolition of slavery in Santo Domingo. Three hundred years after the first black slave had been brought to the island, all were now free.

> *I shall never hesitate between the safety of St. Domingue and my personal happiness*
> —TOUSSAINT L'OUVERTURE

Toussaint as commander in chief of St. Domingue, the French portion of the island of Hispaniola. In 1801, Toussaint invaded and conquered the Spanish part of the island, freeing the slaves.

Leaving his brother Paul as governor of the eastern part of the island, Toussaint returned to St. Domingue, which was devastated after years of constant, total warfare. Few towns had escaped damage, and some were destroyed and deserted. More than one-third of the blacks had been killed; two-thirds of the whites and one-fourth of the mulattoes had died or left the country.

Toussaint knew that his most pressing task was to rebuild the plantations. Most of them had been ruined, along with roads, sugar mills, and irrigation systems. The island's exports had dropped sharply, and so few areas were now under cultivation that many people faced starvation.

He told his people:

> Citizens, it is necessary to consecrate all our moments to the prosperity of St. Domingue. . . . Agriculture is the support of Government; since it is the foundation of Commerce and Wealth. . . . it keeps everybody employed . . . from the moment that every individual becomes useful. . . . disturbances disappear along with idleness. . . . and everyone peaceably enjoys the fruits of his industry.

Toussaint adopted a system called *fermage*, or rent. The government took over the plantations and leased them to people, often generals, who would rebuild and operate them. The operators in turn paid one-fourth of their profits to the workers and provided them with medical care and housing.

To provide workers, Toussaint ordered soldiers to bring unemployed blacks to the plantations. The laborers were bound to the land like medieval serfs. They could not leave the plantations to work elsewhere. Though the system limited the hours of work, in many ways it was very much like slavery. The blacks wished to be free on their own terms; was not this the reason they had fought so long and hard under Toussaint to overthrow their masters? Thus, Toussaint's efforts to rebuild the country's economy ate away at his strongest base of support: the blacks.

Toussaint's generals had the responsibility of making fermage work. Dessalines showed he could

An 1802 rendering of Toussaint. In addition to his administration of military affairs, Toussaint also ran the island's civilian affairs. In one of his programs intended to rebuild St. Domingue's war-shattered agriculture economy, black farmers were ordered to work on plantations under conditions that approached those of slavery.

be as brutal toward blacks as he was toward mulattoes and whites. Punishments for workers on plantations under his control were severe. Those who did not work hard enough were made to run naked through a gauntlet of club-wielding soldiers. A French observer remarked that 10 "free citizens" on Dessalines's plantations did more work than 30 slaves in the old days.

Toussaint needed skilled administrators to direct the work of rebuilding the country. For this reason,

Toussaint at one of his houses. A man whose energy constantly amazed his contemporaries, Toussaint's private life was nearly as full as his public life. Though a Catholic who enjoyed a close relationship with his wife and two sons, he had three mistresses and partook in the Europeanized cultural life of Le Cap.

he encouraged whites who had fled to return. He offered them plantations under the fermage system. Many blacks resented what they felt was his favoritism toward whites. Moise and Dessalines, among others, felt that the blacks alone should be in charge. When Moise was a slave, his eye had been burned out as a punishment. He often said, "I will never love the whites until they give me back my eye."

For a time, Toussaint kept control of the situation. He hoped to use his few remaining years to change his people's future. At his invitation, French priests came to teach. They set up schools where black adults and children learned to read and write. Toussaint brought in artists to teach in the schools, beginning a tradition of Haitian art that continues to this day.

Toussaint — who had been a devout Catholic his entire life and attended mass on a daily basis — restored to the calendar religious holidays, which had been abolished by the Revolution in France. He also tried to suppress the practice of Voodoo and urged former slave couples to formalize their marriage in a church. He urged his officials not to keep mistresses — even though it was common knowledge that he himself had three.

Toussaint rebuilt the towns, restoring the elegance he had seen during the days when French planters lived there. He built a theater in Le Cap where black actors performed the classic works of French playwrights. The city had a new, elegant hotel, where Toussaint himself often dined and enjoyed a game of billiards in the evening.

Some felt that Toussaint was becoming like the French aristocrats of the old regime. He built a grand house for himself and furnished it with such luxuries as marble floors, silk wall hangings, and French furniture. The painted ceilings were based on a pattern that he remembered seeing in the great house at Breda. Each morning, a secretary placed a vase of fresh flowers on his desk.

Toussaint had the final say on everything that happened on the island. He pored over reports from every district, every plantation, taking care that progress was being made. If he saw something that displeased him, he immediately dictated a letter warning the local official in charge to do better.

He regularly held *levées*, or public meetings, at the palace. They were divided between the *grand cercle* and the *petit cercle*. At the first, only his closest advisers, generals, rich whites and mulattoes, and foreign guests were admitted. It was like the court of a French king, except that people of different colors mingled with each other.

On the other hand, any citizen could attend the petit cercle, where the pomp and ceremony were even greater. Trumpets signaled the entrance of Toussaint, resplendent in his full-dress uniform, who walked by those lined up to see him, stopping to talk to those he recognized. People waited for hours to tell him of their problems with husbands,

Napoleon's wife, Empress Josephine. A white Creole born on the nearby French island of Martinique, Josephine corresponded with Toussaint and hosted his two sons, who were attending school in Paris.

wives, children, and neighbors. He saw them all, giving advice and, if necessary, settling quarrels. Toussaint valued these occasions, feeling that through them he could keep in touch with his people.

Even French emigrés wrote to him with their concerns about family or property they had left behind. One surprising correspondent was Napoleon's wife, Josephine. She was a Creole, born on the nearby island of Martinique, but had a relative who owned property on St. Domingue. Toussaint promised to send Josephine her share of the estate's profits and asked in return that she look after his two sons, who were in Paris. Josephine, true to her word, invited the boys to lunch and enjoyed the opportunity to converse in the Creole dialect of her girlhood home. She gave them each a rose from her garden.

Toussaint also owned — or "rented," under the system of fermage — four plantations in the countryside. His wife, who preferred country life to city life, lived at one of them. He visited her often at the plantation, discarding his general's uniform for work clothes and a straw hat. They talked of the day when their sons would return to be masters of plantations where their parents had grown up as slaves.

But Toussaint's times of relaxation were few. He drove himself fiercely. "It is impossible for me to stop," he told an adviser. "Something from me urges me on, and I cannot resist." Five secretaries worked day and night to keep up with his correspondence. He sometimes appeared in his office at three or four in the morning, ready for work.

He never gave up his practice of unexpectedly mounting his horse and riding to a distant village or plantation. There, he would demand to see the record books to find out if the cultivators were being paid. He would visit schools without warning, sit down in a classroom, and ask to hear the children recite their lessons. Were the people contented? Were the children learning? How were the crops this season? His relentless energy continued to astonish all who knew or saw him—as did his secretiveness.

No one knew where or when he might decide to go next. Often, he started in a carriage with an es-

[Toussaint] succeeded, so to speak, in making himself invisible wherever he was and visible where he wasn't; he seemed to have stolen the spontaneity of his movement from a tiger.

—PASCAL
French historian

cort of armed soldiers. Suddenly, he would order a halt, mount one of the horses, and ride off in the opposite direction while the rest of the convoy proceeded as if Toussaint were still with them.

He knew many of the humblest people of the island by name and stopped at the houses of trusted "tanties" — old women who would prepare a native dish such as fish broth or pumpkin soup for him. Sometimes, he stopped in isolated spots to bathe in a stream, no doubt remembering the days of his boyhood, when he was the Centaur of the Plains. Destiny had put all the hopes of St. Domingue on his shoulders.

For a time, St. Domingue began to rebuild and was at peace. But the outside world would not let the island alone. The British were rumored to be on the verge of negotiating peace with Napoleon. Soon, Toussaint knew, Napoleon would be free to reestablish French control on the island.

In the spring of 1801, Toussaint called an assembly of hand-picked officials to draft a constitution for the island. Toussaint said pointedly that the island's interests were "different from those of France." Equally important, none of the members of the assembly was black except Toussaint.

Toussaint (at left in profile) leading black soldiers against British troops. Britain's military effort in the West Indies, which cost 40,000 British lives, was suspended in 1799 when Britain signed a pact with Toussaint. But in 1801, a British treaty with Napoleon prompted him to bolster St. Domingue's claim to autonomy.

A 20th-century painting by a Haitian artist shows Toussaint reading the island's constitution, which he promulgated in 1802. The document guaranteed the rights of all citizens regardless of color and established an elected assembly but allowed Toussaint to retain full dictatorial powers nevertheless.

The constitution abolished slavery forever. It declared that each citizen of the island, regardless of color, was eligible for any occupation or government post. It preserved the rights of former plantation owners who were absent from the colony "for whatever reason."

Despite the existence of the assembly, Toussaint remained all-powerful. "Remember," he said, "there is but one Toussaint in St. Domingue, and at his name, all must tremble." The government was in effect an absolute dictatorship headed by the governor, who controlled the officials, police, army, and even the church. Toussaint was named governor-for-life, with the power to name his successor if he ever chose to step down.

Was Toussaint declaring St. Domingue's independence? Not in so many words, but there was no mention of France in the island's constitution. Toussaint asked the only remaining French commissioner, Colonel Vincent, to take the constitution to Napoleon.

Vincent tried to persuade Toussaint to withdraw the constitution; Napoleon's response, he counseled, could only be outrage. But Toussaint insisted, shouting insults which hurt Vincent so deeply that when he wrote his memoirs, he said he could not repeat them.

In St. Domingue, others read the constitution with amazement and anger. Knowing that it must bring war with France, whites once again began packing to leave the island. What hurt Toussaint most was the reaction of the blacks. Moise snorted, "Who does he think he is, King of Haiti?" Moise had not fought so long for freedom only to have it taken away — even by Toussaint, who had given him a general's rank.

Moise spread the rumor among the cultivators that Toussaint was planning to restore slavery. He led those who joined him in raids against the hated plantations, beginning the cycle of destruction and civil war once again.

Dessalines and Christophe had their own doubts about Toussaint's action, but they remained loyal. They marched their troops into Moise's district and seized him and many of his men.

This time, Toussaint turned his wrath against his own people. He had some of the prisoners brought to Le Cap and assembled in the main square. Toussaint gave pistols to the officers who had turned against him and ordered them to kill themselves. This they did, grateful to avoid the fate that awaited others. Forty others were tied to the mouths of cannons and blasted to bits. The scene was repeated at two other towns. While Toussaint watched, his soldiers bayonetted a thousand cultivators who had left the plantations to follow Moise. Moise himself was shot by a firing squad.

All who followed Toussaint trembled. He had proved that he would tolerate no opposition. But a greater threat to Toussaint loomed across the ocean in France. When Napoleon finally attacked St. Domingue, its people fought back not because they loved Toussaint, but because they feared him.

Toussaint is a brilliant officer; indefatigable in action; cautious in his proceedings; and is not careless and negligent.
—CAPTAIN WICKHAM
American sea captain

7

"This Gilded African"

When Colonel Vincent presented the constitution to Napoleon, the first consul flew into a rage. "This gilded African!" he shouted, referring to Toussaint. "I will not rest until I have torn the epaulettes [an officer's shoulder decorations] off every nigger in the colonies."

Napoleon's anger caused him to banish Vincent to the island of Elba. Ironically, 13 years later, Vincent would welcome Napoleon himself — by then a captive of his European enemies — to the island prison.

From Elba, Vincent wrote Napoleon a long letter, pleading for St. Domingue, "Sire, leave it alone!" He gave a first-hand appraisal of Toussaint:

> God destined this man to govern. Races melt beneath his hand. . . . It is the strictest truth to say that he is everywhere. . . . He is the absolute master of the island and nothing can counteract his wishes, whatever they may be.

But Napoleon was not deterred. "I am for the whites because I am white," he said. "I have no other reason. That one is enough." His support for the restoration of white supremacy on the island was

You cannot keep Toussaint at too great a distance from the sea nor in a place too sure. The man has fanaticized this country to such a degree that his appearance would set everything once more aflame.
—GENERAL LECLERC
July 1802

Toussaint receives Napoleon's letter, brought by Toussaint's sons Isaac and Placide. In the letter, which Toussaint took as an attempt at deception, Napoleon offered liberty for St. Domingue's blacks in exchange for the Toussaint's agreement to govern the island with Leclerc.

reinforced when he asked his advisers whether the profits from St. Domingue's plantations would be greater with slavery or without it. They responded that slavery was the more profitable system. "Then," Napoleon said, "the sooner we return to that system the better."

He had other reasons for wanting to destroy Toussaint's hold on St. Domingue. He had plans for world conquest, and St. Domingue was the stepping-stone to the continent of North America. West of the United States, the vast French territory of Louisiana awaited exploitation.

In October 1801, Napoleon made peace with England, and the British blockade that had kept French troopships from reaching St. Domingue was lifted. At the same time the United States also turned its back on Toussaint. Thomas Jefferson, the young nation's third president, held slaves on his Virginia plantation and was warned by his fellow slaveholders that Toussaint's rebellion must be stopped before it spread to the United States. Taking heed, the Jefferson administration brought its alliance with St. Domingue to an end. Toussaint was alone.

Napoleon was now ready to move. He appointed his brother-in-law, General Victor-Emmanuel Leclerc, to lead a French army into St. Domingue. In secret instructions, Napoleon told Leclerc exactly how to proceed. First, take the coastal towns. From there, spread out to defeat any organized resistance. Finally, restore slavery when control of the island is secure.

Deceit was part of Napoleon's plan. "In the first phase," he wrote to Leclerc, "negotiate with Toussaint, promise him everything he asks — in order to gain possession of the key points." He named black generals, including Christophe and Maurepas, that he thought could be persuaded to abandon Toussaint: "In the first phase, confirm them in their rank and position. In the last phase, send them to France." Toussaint, he advised, must be encouraged to come to Le Cap or Port-au-Prince to declare his loyalty to France. When he did, "without scandal or violence but with honors and consideration, he must be [put aboard a ship] and sent to France."

To offer some incentive to draw Toussaint into Leclerc's camp, Napoleon used Toussaint's sons. He sent Placide and Isaac (then 21 and 16 years old, respectively) with General Leclerc, promising them they would soon be reunited with their father. He also gave the boys an enameled box containing a letter for their father. In the letter, Napoleon showered Toussaint with praises and promised he could "count without reserve on our esteem."

Leclerc spent the fall of 1801 preparing an invasion fleet, consisting of 67 ships carrying more than 21,000 soldiers. Leclerc's second-in-command, General Rochambeau, was, at 46, the eldest of the commanders. All were seasoned veterans of Napoleon's campaigns. The fleet also carried André Rigaud, Alexandre Pétion, and other mulatto leaders who had fled the island. Napoleon thought that they could be useful in rousing the mulattoes against Toussaint. But Napoleon privately told Leclerc that if there proved to be no need for them, the mulatto leaders should be taken to Africa and left on the beach.

Leclerc's wife, Pauline — Napoleon's sister — also went along. She expected to set up her own little court on the island, and so she brought artists, musicians, maids, and trunks of lavish dresses.

A 1799 American cartoon drawn in reaction to the abolition of slavery in St. Domingue. As a top-hatted Briton and a uniformed Frenchman encourage St. Domingue slaves to burn Washington, D.C., an American slave drops his tools and runs away. U.S. fears that the slave revolt would spread led it to break off relations with Toussaint in 1801.

Monticello, the Virginia mansion of U.S. president Thomas Jefferson. Jefferson, himself a slaveholder, ended U.S. government support for Toussaint after being urged to do so by other American slaveholders.

Toussaint had already made preparations against an attack. He stored military supplies throughout the mountains of St. Domingue that he knew so well. He spread his men along the coast, leaving the cities garrisoned with soldiers under his most trusted generals. He saw, to his sorrow, that many whites looked forward to the arrival of Napoleon's men, despite Toussaint's kindness toward them. He would make them pay.

On February 2, 1802, the first ships arrived off Le Cap. Toussaint and his staff sat on their horses on a bluff overlooking the harbor. They watched ship after ship lay anchor. Others passed by Le Cap, heading for other parts of the island. Though he was seeing less than half of the total French force, Toussaint muttered, "We are doomed. All France has come to invade us." Yet he would prove the truth of his warning — the blacks loved their liberty too much to surrender without a fight.

General Leclerc came ashore and met Christophe, the commander of Toussaint's troops at Le Cap. Toussaint did not reveal his presence, wanting to sound out his enemy's intentions first. Leclerc demanded that the French troops be allowed to come ashore and occupy the city. He promised Christophe that the blacks' freedom would be preserved. Christophe warned that the city would be burned if Leclerc tried to take it by force.

Toussaint knew that Leclerc was already sending men ashore east and west of the city, hoping to trap Christophe's forces inside. If Toussaint waited too long, the city would be surrounded. He gave the order to destroy Le Cap. On February 4, Christophe went to his own fine mansion and set fire to it. Throughout Le Cap, other soldiers put to the torch all that Toussaint had rebuilt during his brief time as ruler.

As the flames rose, Christophe and Toussaint led their men south. When Leclerc's forces came ashore, there were fewer than 60 houses still standing. That was to be the fate of much of St. Domingue. As Leclerc wrote Napoleon, "Toussaint and his generals appear to me to have decided to burn down the colony and entomb themselves under the ruins before surrendering their empire."

Indeed, Toussaint's only chance at victory was to destroy every possible source of supply or support for Leclerc. He had seen, when he fought the British, that European troops were weakened by yellow fever and the unfamiliar heat of the tropics. If he could hold out long enough, St. Domingue itself would defeat Leclerc.

"Burn everything," he wrote to Dessalines. "Block the roads, pollute the wells with corpses and dead horses. Leave nothing white behind you." Dessalines needed no encouragement to turn against the whites. He told his men: "Cut off their heads! Burn down their houses!" He left piles of white bodies behind him as a warning to the French troops that followed.

Leclerc followed Napoleon's advice and promised Toussaint honors and a high military post if he surrendered. He sent Toussaint's sons to their father with a letter from Napoleon promising Toussaint an end to the invasion if he declared his loyalty to France. Toussaint embraced his sons when they arrived in his camp. With them came a French priest named Coisnon, who had been their teacher. Coisnon, on orders from Leclerc, reminded Toussaint of his duty to France. Toussaint read Napoleon's letter and remarked that while Napoleon offered peace, Leclerc had brought war.

Toussaint's sons urged him to meet with Leclerc, who had shown them kindness. They told him of their luncheons with Napoleon's wife, Josephine. Toussaint saw that in their years away from the island they had indeed become like young French gentlemen. He did not want them to share the suffering that the war would bring. He gave them the choice of remaining with him, or of going back to Leclerc. The elder, Placide, declared he would never leave his father. Isaac went back, though he would later return.

Leclerc declared Toussaint a rebel against France and issued proclamations telling the blacks to surrender. He insisted he had no wish to take away their freedom. It was part of Napoleon's plan — promise anything to gain victory.

But Leclerc was already running into difficulties. His men took many of the coastal cities — as Napoleon had planned — but the resistance inland was unexpectedly fierce. Only 2 weeks after their arrival, 2,000 French soldiers already lay ill from tropical diseases. Toussaint had retreated into the mountains, counting on the arrival of the rainy season to defend him. "Why have so many ships crossed the ocean," he told his men, "if not to throw you again into chains?"

General Rochambeau led a force in pursuit of Toussaint. In a narrow pass through the mountains, called Ravine-à-Couleuvre (Ravine of the Serpent), Toussaint assembled his men. His family was in hiding not far away, and he ordered them to flee. On the 23rd of February, Rochambeau launched his attack. For six hours, the battle seesawed back and forth. But the superior weapons of the French could not be overcome, and Toussaint was forced to withdraw with heavy losses. The French forces on the island outnumbered his own by two-to-one. He could not afford many battles of this kind.

Napoleon's plan to lure Toussaint's followers away from him began to bear fruit. Maurepas, one of Toussaint's most trusted generals, surrendered. Both he and most of his men volunteered to fight with Leclerc. Leclerc named Maurepas a general of the army of France, but within a year the French would execute him.

In late 1801, Napoleon sent a force of more than 20,000 soldiers, commanded by his brother-in-law General Victor-Emmanuel Leclerc (pictured here), to invade St. Domingue. The force, whose mission was to retake St. Domingue from the blacks and restore slavery, arrived in early 1802.

Toussaint, meanwhile, adopted the tactics of guerrilla warfare. He sent small bands of men to harass the French, destroy their supplies, and then retreat back into the forests and mountains, like the maroons of old.

Dessalines's forces adopted more conventional tactics. They occupied an old British fort at La Crête-à-Pierrot, which commanded the pass into the mountains. From there Dessalines could see French troops marching toward him on the plains far below. The fort's cannons blazed forth, pounding the French. La Crête became a symbol of resistance. Dessalines rallied his men by waving a torch by the powder magazine, declaring that he would blow the fort up rather than surrender.

The French and their mulatto allies drew up their own cannons and bombarded the fort. Alexandre Pétion, now serving the French, put Dessalines on the receiving end of the barrage he had suffered at Jacmel. The besiegers knew that without further supplies of food and ammunition, the fort's defenders would have to yield. French soldiers surrounding the fort could hear the black soldiers inside singing "The Marseillaise," the anthem of the French Revolution. A French general reported that his own men began to wonder about the justice of their cause.

As starvation overcame the defenders, the fort had to be abandoned. Even then, Dessalines managed

Le Cap burns after retreating black defenders set it to the torch in February 1802. Leclerc's forces took possession of the burned-out city and later found much of the countryside burned as well, as Toussaint ordered his men to destroy crops and livestock rather than have it fall into the hands of the superior French invasion army.

French soldiers battle black troops at Ravine-à-Couleuvre in February 1802. By May 7, the French invasion army and its mulatto allies forced Toussaint to surrender.

to save most of his men by having them slip through the French lines at night. The French general admitted that the retreat was "a remarkable feat of arms. We had more than 12,000 men surrounding him (yet) he got away . . . and left us only his dead and wounded."

In April 1802, Christophe, the other black general whom Napoleon thought might be swayed, broke off fighting and met with Leclerc. After he received a general's commission and promises of freedom for all the former slaves, he surrendered.

Scholars disagree as to whether Christophe was a traitor. Some claim that he was acting with Toussaint's blessing, as a test to see how Leclerc would react. Toussaint himself was already negotiating by messenger with Leclerc, and only 11 days after Christophe's surrender, he came to Le Cap with a bodyguard of 400 men.

At the first meeting between the two commanders, Leclerc came forward with his arms open for an embrace that Toussaint avoided. Not deterred, Leclerc said, "General, allow me to show my admiration for the way you have shouldered the responsibility of the government of St. Domingue." Toussaint asked him why he had come to a peaceful country bearing a sword. Leclerc waved this off and said, "Between us we will restore the island and make it blossom again."

At this point Toussaint saw his favorite horse, Bel Argent, which had been captured by one of Leclerc's generals, being ridden by a black officer who had deserted to the French. His eyes narrowed in anger. Those who rode with him knew this was a bad sign.

Leclerc brought Toussaint to dinner with a group of French generals. Leclerc told Napoleon later that Toussaint showed no appetite. When offered wine, he asked for water. The black general, fearing poison, ate only a little cheese and even then cut the slab of cheese open and took his portion from the inside.

Leclerc tried to make small talk about military matters. He asked Toussaint how he would have gotten his supplies if the war continued. Toussaint said, "Why, General, I would have taken them from you." When the negotiations began, Leclerc offered generous terms — continued freedom for all the blacks and commissions for Toussaint and his officers. Toussaint declined a commission for himself, saying he wished to retire to his plantation at Ennery. Finally, on May 7, 1802, Toussaint agreed to surrender. The French would now resume their control over the island.

Toussaint was forced to surrender because the French had grown too powerful for his forces to stop. Two months earlier, Napoleon had signed the Treaty of Amiens, which for the time being ended France's war in Europe. Now, he could bring any number of troops to St. Domingue, which by itself could not defeat France.

Toussaint L'Ouverture withdrew from public affairs and settled down to a simple life with his wife at Ennery. Although his informants kept him apprised of developments throughout the island, he made no move against the French.

Even so, he would not be allowed to live out the remainder of his life in peace.

8

The Trunk of the Tree of Liberty

Leclerc was not about to let Toussaint remain on the island. He felt that if he could get rid of Toussaint once and for all, the blacks would lose the only leader who could unite them. Leclerc had one of his generals, Jean-Baptiste Brunet, invite Toussaint to his headquarters for a meeting. Toussaint was probably warned that this was a trap, but he went anyway. He may have been overconfident that his allies would immediately avenge any attempt to capture him.

When he came to Brunet's headquarters, 10 officers immediately surrounded him, their sabers and pistols drawn. Toussaint drew his own sword, but there were too many to fight, and he put it down. His captors bound him with ropes and took him to Gonaïves, a nearby port town. A ship was waiting, and as soon as Toussaint was on board, it set sail for Le Cap. There, Toussaint's wife and two sons were brought aboard. All of them were to be taken to France.

The parallels have their contrasts. Toussaint fought for liberty; Bonaparte fought for himself. Toussaint gained fame and power by leading an oppressed and injured race to the successful vindication of their rights; Bonaparte made himself a name by . . . supplanting liberty and destroying nationalities.
—REVEREND JOHN R. BEARD
Toussaint biographer

The arrest of Toussaint L'Ouverture in mid-1802. Napoleon ordered Toussaint's arrest and imprisonment to remove the focus of black opposition to the restoration of slavery in St. Domingue.

95

As the ship left St. Domingue, Toussaint took a last look at the island where he was born. He turned to his French captors and said, "In overthrowing me you have cut down in St. Domingue only the trunk of the tree of liberty. It will spring up again from the roots, for they are many and they are deep." Two weeks after Toussaint's surrender to Leclerc, Napoleon signed a secret order restoring slavery within the French colonies in the West Indies. Other orders, which came from Paris the following month, stripped the mulattoes of the equal rights granted them in the early days of the French Revolution. With France's treasury drained by its European wars, Napoleon clearly intended the French Caribbean colonies to return to their old, slave-based profitability.

But on St. Domingue, Leclerc did not try to carry out the orders. More than three-fourths of his men were dead or ill from various tropical diseases, including two of Leclerc's generals, who had died of yellow fever; Leclerc himself was suffering from malaria. It was impossible for him and his badly depleted forces to make any attempt to reimpose slavery in the colony.

The French commander on the nearby island of Martinique, however, did carry out Napoleon's orders to restore slavery. When word of the developments on Martinique spread to St. Domingue, the cultivators on the plantations once again began their nighttime meetings. All through the summer, Leclerc sent frantic letters to Napoleon pleading for replacements for his stricken troops. Napoleon ignored him.

To at least one person, however, life on the island was a pleasant interlude. Every evening, Leclerc's wife, Pauline, held parties for the wealthy white planters and traders who still remained in Le Cap. They danced away the night, while deep within the mountains drums called the blacks to fight for freedom. Visitors were shocked at the shameless way Pauline flirted with the men. One of her husband's young aides performed the duty of massaging her feet during her afternoon naps.

France's hold on the island weakened. Dessalines and Christophe, aware that Toussaint had been im-

Fort de Joux, in the French Alps along the border with Switzerland. Toussaint was taken by ship from St. Domingue and imprisoned here on August 25, 1802.

prisoned in France, once more decided to lead the rebellion. The ranks of the rebels grew daily, and shortly a rebel force was heading for the tortured city of Le Cap. Leclerc, hardly able to rise from his bed, wrote a last frantic letter to Napoleon. In it he wrote that the only course of action was "to exterminate all the blacks . . . women as well as men, except for children under 12." Unless Napoleon sent 12,000 fresh troops to carry the mass slaughter, "St. Domingue is lost forever."

Two weeks after Toussaint's surrender, Napoleon signed a secret order restoring slavery in the French West Indies. However, Leclerc's forces on the island — badly depleted by yellow fever — did not attempt to carry out the order for fear of another black uprising.

Leclerc died in early November 1802. His replacement, General Rochambeau, faced a virtually hopeless situation. Although the French held the coastal cities, they could offer little resistance against the growing rebellion. Napoleon sent only a few fresh troops, and his order to reinstate the antimulatto laws gave the rebels new allies. For the first time, blacks and mulattoes united against the whites.

Toussaint had never been able to effect such an alliance; indeed, his hatred of the mulattoes had sometimes led him to order appalling massacres. Undoubtedly his absence was one of the reasons blacks and mulattoes were finally able to unite.

Toussaint may not have been aware of events in St. Domingue once the ship transporting him to France had sailed from the island's waters. On the voyage, Toussaint was confined to quarters and not allowed to see his family. When the ship reached

France, he dictated a letter protesting his arrest and declaring that none of his family were responsible for his actions. Napoleon nevertheless ordered that all of them be confined separately in prisons in different parts of France. Toussaint was permitted to embrace his wife and children for one last time on the deck of the ship. Sailors who witnessed the scene wept along with them.

A coach with armed guards was waiting to take Toussaint across France to Fort de Joux, a forbidding place in the Jura Mountains on the border of Switzerland. Toussaint, who had lived all his life in the sunny tropics, was now in a region of snow and cold. The fort's stone walls, built during the Crusades, were 12 feet thick and would be like blocks of ice once the winter arrived.

General Rochambeau, who took command of French forces in St. Domingue after Leclerc died of malaria in November 1802. After the imprisonment of Toussaint, the island's mulattoes allied with the blacks; in the face of a united black-mulatto army, Rochambeau's military situation was hopeless.

All the way from St. Domingue, Toussaint had worn his French general's uniform. Now, at Napoleon's order, it was stripped from his body. He was given the second-hand uniform of a private. Dirty and disheveled, he was taken deep within the fort to a tiny cell whose sole window had been bricked up; only a sliver of daylight shone through. The cell contained a bed, two wooden chairs, a small table, and a commode. He was given food and firewood to burn in the small open fireplace, but on Napoleon's orders he was never allowed to leave the cell, not even for exercise.

A servant from the island remained with Toussaint for a short time. He later wrote, "On going in there I thought I was entering a cave. The doors were only opened at meal-times." He reported that Toussaint often talked of his family, fearing what Napoleon would do to them.

Toussaint entered his cell on August 25, 1802. A month and two days later, an aide of Napoleon's arrived to find him already "trembling with cold and illness, suffering greatly and having difficulty in speaking."

Toussaint had aroused Napoleon's interest by hinting in a letter that he had important information to disclose. Napoleon had heard rumors that Toussaint had a large treasure of plundered gold and jewels hidden somewhere on the island. However, Toussaint soon made his real purpose clear to Napoleon's aide. He had written a memoir of his life and a letter to his wife. He asked the aide to give the memoir to Napoleon, as proof that he never betrayed France, and to send the letter to his wife, wherever she might be.

The memoir contained a plea for a court-martial to decide whether or not he had committed treason against France. Toussaint told Napoleon that he relied "upon your justice and integrity." The words were wasted. Napoleon had no intention of allowing Toussaint a trial.

The letter to his wife declared his affection and asked why he had not heard from her. She never received the letter. Napoleon kept it.

The commander of Fort de Joux was ordered to report all of Toussaint's requests directly to Napo-

I have to reproach myself with the attempt made upon the colony during the consulship. The design of reducing it by force was a great error. I ought to have been satisfied with governing it through the medium of Toussaint.

—NAPOLEON
on the failure of France's attempt to regain control of the colony

The last page from the memoir written by Toussaint in his prison cell during the last weeks of his life. This page contains a plea for mercy to Napoleon, who was to pass judgment "on a man more unlucky than guilty."

leon. When Toussaint asked for bandanas to wrap around his head as protection against the cold, the request was denied. Napoleon was told that Toussaint appeared to enjoy the use of his prized pocket watch, a beautiful object decorated with jewels. He ordered that it be taken from Toussaint, along with all his other personal effects. When Toussaint persisted in writing letters pleading for a trial and asking for news of his wife, Napoleon ordered that Toussaint's pen and paper be taken as well.

The winter was a hard one for the prisoner kept alone in the cell at Fort de Joux. He was unaware that André Rigaud, his old rival, shared a similar fate in another cell of the prison. The commandant of the fort visited Toussaint daily. In his reports to Napoleon, the commandant said that the man con-

Toussaint's body, discovered in his cell on April 7, 1803. On Napoleon's orders, he had not been fed or given firewood for four days.

tinually complained about his treatment but never spoke of St. Domingue.

When Toussaint's health grew worse, the commandant refused to allow a doctor to visit him. That would be useless, the commandant wrote, for "the constitution of Negroes bears no resemblance to that of Europeans."

At the beginning of April, the commandant had to leave the fort on a mission. He gave orders that while he was gone, no one was to enter the prisoner's cell. For four days, Toussaint received no more food or firewood. When the commandant returned to the cell on April 7, 1803, he found Toussaint seated in one of the wooden chairs, with his head resting against the cold fireplace. He was dead.

One month later, back on St. Domingue, Dessalines and Christophe met with mulatto leaders and proclaimed the island's independence from France. Dessalines, who was chosen to be the new nation's leader, took the blue, white, and red French flag and ripped out the white panel. There was to be no white in the flag of independent St. Domingue.

The combined blacks and mulattoes found that the disease-decimated French forces could not stand before them. They took town after town, sweeping through both south and north. By October 1803, the French held only two cities.

One of them was Le Cap, where Rochambeau was holed up with 5,000 French soldiers. On November 18, 1803, Dessalines, with 16,000 men, took the last of the outlying forts around Le Cap. The fort stood on the former plantation of Breda, where Toussaint, now buried in Fort de Joux, had been born.

Rochambeau could not hold out. He sent an officer under a flag of truce to beg Dessalines to give him 10 days to get his men aboard ships in the harbor. Dessalines agreed, and on November 29, his men marched unopposed into the town. Less than a week later, the other French-held garrison sur-

On January 1, 1804, St. Domingue was declared the independent republic of Haiti, but the new nation soon broke apart under the strain of racial turmoil. Alexandre Pétion (pictured here) became the leader of a mulatto republic in the south of Haiti, which warred constantly with the black kingdom in the north.

The Citadel, a fortress in northern Haiti built by King Henri Christophe at the cost of thousands of laborers' lives in the 1820s. The fortress was built to defend against a possible return of the vanquished French, who for decades after Haiti became independent, threatened to send an invasion force to retake their former colony.

rendered, and St. Domingue was at last a land of free and independent people.

On receiving the news, Napoleon raged, "Damn sugar! Damn coffee! Damn colonies!" In December 1803, with his treasury depleted by the disastrous military effort in St. Domingue and his continental armies badly in need of funds for their wars against the combined kingdoms of Europe, Napoleon was forced to sell the vast Louisiana Territory to the United States. Napoleon had lost not only St. Domingue but also his dream of building a new French empire in North America.

On January 1, 1804, in the town of Gonaïves, to the roll of drums and the sound of trumpets, Dessalines stood on a platform decorated with the two-colored flag and declared the establishment of a new nation: Haiti. "We must live free or we must die," read Haiti's declaration of independence, a document that one of Dessalines' aides said was written with "blood for ink and a bayonet for a pen."

"*Vive l'indépendance!*" shouted Dessalines in Creole, a language that all who had gathered to hear him in Gonaïves's central plaza could understand. Cannons roared and church bells pealed as the

A village in rural Haiti in the 1980s. Toussaint led the first slave revolt in history to result in the founding of an independent nation and inspired millions around the world, but many of the problems he encountered — and helped to create — continue to plague Haiti today. Poverty, political terror, and deep hatred between blacks and mulattoes still mark the second-oldest independent nation in the Western Hemisphere.

crowd repeated, "Long live independence!" They had witnessed the birth of the world's first black republic, the second independent nation in the New World, and the first nation anywhere to have gained its freedom as the result of a slave rebellion.

The Haitian republic did not last long. Later in the year, when Dessalines heard that Napoleon had been declared emperor, he adopted the same title for himself. He was crowned Jacques I seven weeks before Napoleon's official coronation. Two years later, Dessalines was killed in a new civil war between blacks and mulattoes as the island's old hatreds flared anew. Henri Christophe took control of the north, and the mulatto Alexandre Pétion, the south. The country was not reunited until 1822. Santo Domingo gained its independence from Haiti in 1844, and the island remains two countries today: Creole- and French-speaking Haiti in the west and the Spanish-speaking Dominican Republic in the east. And as the 20th century draws to a close, Haiti is still wracked by violence, oppression, poverty, and mutual distrust between blacks and mulattoes.

Toussaint L'Ouverture did not live to see his country's independence, but his leadership had made it possible. Today he is a revered figure not only for the people of Haiti but for blacks throughout the world. In the 19th century his example inspired slaves in bondage throughout the Caribbean and in the United States; in the 20th century, African leaders studied his life for inspiration in their struggle against the European nations that had colonized their continent.

Those who love freedom have always admired Toussaint. Even during his life he was famed throughout much of the world, and while he was freezing in his prison cell his story inspired the great English poet William Wordsworth to memorialize his suffering in a sonnet. "Toussaint," Wordsworth wrote, "the most unhappy Man of Men."

Toussaint was truly remarkable. A man with no formal education, he showed extraordinary gifts of leadership. From undisciplined bands of rebellious slaves, he formed an army that defeated the three greatest nations of Europe. In the complex diplomatic game with the French, Spanish, British, and Americans, as well as with the many groups that made up St. Domingue's complicated society, he maneuvered skillfully to win favorable agreements. In the midst of devastation, he worked to try to establish a strong economic base for his country. In a world that accepted racism and thought blacks inferior, Toussaint showed that he and the men and women he led were the equals of any statesman, diplomat, general, or army that stood against them.

The American Revolution and the French Revolution showed that kings were no longer able to govern without the consent of their subjects. The Haitian Revolution showed the world that a people enslaved could rise up to throw off its chains. Toussaint, the leader of that revolution, was in the words of the Abbé Raynal, "the hero who . . . established the rights of the human race."

There's not a breathing of the common wind that will forget thee: thou hast great allies: Thy friends are exultations, agonies, And love, and man's unconquerable mind.
—WILLIAM WORDSWORTH
lines urging the imprisoned Toussaint to find solace in his immortality

Further Reading

Anthony, Suzanne. *Haiti.* New York: Chelsea House, 1989.

Beard, John R. *The Life of Toussaint L'Ouverture.* Westport, CT: Negro Universities Press, 1970.

Heinl, Robert D., and Nancy Gordon Heinl. *Written In Blood: The Story of the Haitian People.* Boston, MA: Houghton Mifflin, 1978.

James, C. L. R. *The Black Jacobins: Toussaint L'Ouverture and the San Domingo Revolution.* New York: Vintage, 1963.

Lewis, Gordon K. *Main Currents in Caribbean Thought.* Baltimore, MD: Johns Hopkins University Press, 1983.

Ott, Thomas O. *The Haitian Revolution: 1789–1804.* Knoxville: University of Tennessee Press, 1973.

Parkinson, Wenda. *This Gilded African: Toussaint L'Ouverture.* London: Quartet Books, 1971.

Parry, J. H., and Philip M. Sherlock. *A Short History of the West Indies.* London: Macmillan, 1971.

Scherman, Katherine. *The Slave Who Freed Haiti.* New York: Random House, 1954.

Steward, T. G. *The Haitian Revolution: 1791 to 1804.* New York: Russell & Russell, 1971.

Syme, Ronald. *Toussaint: The Black Liberator.* New York: William Morrow, 1971.

Tyson, George F. *Toussaint L'Ouverture.* Englewood Cliffs, NJ: Prentice-Hall, 1973.

Williams, Eric. *From Columbus to Castro: The History of the Caribbean, 1492–1969.* New York: Harper & Row, 1970.

Chronology

ca. 1744	Toussaint born on Breda plantation in French Caribbean colony of St. Domingue
1758	Mackandal slave uprising begins
1789	French Revolution begins
1790	Ogé's rebellion takes place
Aug. 22, 1791	Outbreak of slave revolt, which Toussaint joins one month later
Apr. 14, 1792	French Assembly grants full rights and privileges to all mulattoes
1793	French commissioner Sonthonax proclaims emancipation of slaves; Toussaint's army occupies central St. Domingue
1794	French National Convention abolishes slavery
1795	Toussaint's army drives Spanish from St. Domingue
1796	Toussaint named lieutenant governor of St. Domingue
1797—98	Toussaint made commander in chief of French armies in the colony; forces Sonthonax to return to France; British and French forces evacuate St. Domingue, leaving Toussaint in control of the colony
1799	Civil war begins between blacks under Toussaint and mulattoes under Rigaud
1800	Toussaint defeats Rigaud, proclaims forced labor policy
1801	Toussaint captures Spanish half of island; promulgates constitution; puts down rebellion led by nephew
1802	French under Leclerc invade; Toussaint and Dessalines surrender; Toussaint arrested
1803	Toussaint dies in prison in France
Jan. 1, 1804	Haiti declared independent republic

Index

PICTURE CREDITS

Bettmann Archive: pp. 16, 45, 46, 49, 57, 74, 92; Bibliothèque nationale, Paris: p. 84; Culver Pictures: pp. 50, 65; David/Scala/Art Resource: p. 72; De Florio/Art Resource: p. 26; Giraudon/Art Resource/Musée Carnavalet: p. 30; Haiti National Tourist Office: p. 104; Jean-Loup Charmet, Paris: pp. 20, 23, 38, 40, 42–43, 69, 71, 87, 91; Library of Congress: pp. 32–33, 79, 98, 99; Courtesy of the Director, National Army Museum, London: p. 62; The National Portrait Gallery: p. 66; New York Public Library/Astor, Lenox and Tilden Foundations: pp. 88, 101; Organization of American States: p. 106; Roger-Viollet, Paris: pp. 2, 21, 27, 29, 34, 36, 58, 81, 90, 97; Schomburg Center for Research in Black Culture, New York Public Library, Astor, Lenox and Tilden Foundations: pp. 12, 15, 18, 19, 28, 35, 53, 60, 77, 78, 82, 94, 102, 103; Gary Tong: p. 54

Dorothy and Thomas Hoobler have written many award-winning books for children and young adults. Their books have been included on the New York Public Library's annual Books for the Teen Age list. The Hooblers have written numerous books in the Chelsea House series WORLD LEADERS—PAST & PRESENT, including *Stalin* and *Cleopatra.* They reside in New York City with their daughter, Ellen.

Arthur M. Schlesinger, jr., taught history at Harvard for many years and is currently Albert Schweitzer Professor of the Humanities at City University of New York. He is the author of numerous highly praised works in American history and has twice been awarded the Pulitzer Prize. He served in the White House as special assistant to Presidents Kennedy and Johnson.

ACKNOWLEDGMENT

The authors would like to thank Julie Hetrick, Serge LaFontant, and the New York Public Library staff for their support and assistance.